Odd Man Out?

Myth and Realities in the British Approach to the European Union

Edited by Brendan Donnelly
and Henning Meyer

First published in 2009 by Forumpress

Forumpress
c/o The Global Policy Institute
London Metropolitan University
31 Jewry Street
London EC3N 2EY, UK

ISBN: 978-0-9554975-9-9

A catalogue record for this book is available from the British Library.

For further information on Forumpress, visit our website: www.forumpress.co.uk

Design and Layout: Ben Eldridge www.beneldridge.co.uk

Printed by Lightning Source www.lightningsource.com

Contents

Notes on Contributors

John Cooke is a Federal Trust Council member and chairman of the Liberalisation of Trade Services (LOTIS) Committee of International Financial Services London (IFSL). An economic consultant, he was formerly an official at the DTI and UK Representation in Brussels. He writes in a personal capacity.

Brendan Donnelly is the Director of the Federal Trust for Education and Research. He is a former Member of the European Parliament (1994-1999). He gained a double first in Classics at Oxford and later worked in the Foreign Office, the European Parliament and the European Commission.

Nadine El-Enany is a PhD researcher in the Law Department at the European University Institute, Florence, and teaches at the London School of Economics (LSE). Her research specialisation is the growing restrictiveness of European law and refugee policy.

Frédéric Lerais joined the Bureau of European Policy Advisors, European Commission, on secondment from the French Labour Ministry in 2005. He specialises in issues related to labour markets, employment policies and social protection. An economist-statistician with a degree from ENSAE, he has worked for one of the major French institutes for economic studies (OFCE).

Roger Liddle chairs the international centre-left think tank Policy Network. He also chairs the UK Government's New Industry, New Jobs, Universities and Skills advisory panel, as well as holding a visiting fellowship at the LSE's European Institute. Until October 2007 he was economic advisor to the European Commission president and, before that, European advisor to Tony Blair.

Peter Luff chairs the European Movement UK and is chief executive officer of Action for a Global Climate Community. He is also a trustee of the Coalition for an International Court for the Environment and the European Multi-cultural Foundation, and a council member of the World Federalist Movement. He has been the assistant director of Amnesty International UK.

Henning Meyer is senior research fellow and head of the European Programme at the Global Policy Institute at London Metropolitan University. Specialising in social democracy, European integration, social and economic policy and transatlantic economic relations, he was also visiting fellow at the School for Industrial and Labor Relations at Cornell University.

Eiko Thielemann is a senior lecturer in European Politics and Policy in the Department of Government and the European Institute at the LSE, where he is programme director and academic chair of the LSE Migration Studies Unit. His research focuses particularly on asylum and immigration issues.

Richard Whitman joined the Department of European Studies and Modern Languages, University of Bath, in 2006 from Chatham House where he was head of the European Programme and senior fellow. Previously he was professor of European Studies at the University of Westminster. He currently chairs the EU Neighbourhood Forum for the Brussels-based European Policy Centre.

Preface

This collection of essays is based upon the speeches given at a series of conferences on 'British Exceptionalism', jointly organised by the Federal Trust and the Global Policy Institute between September 2008 and May 2009. We should like to thank all the contributors to this volume and our colleagues at the Federal Trust and the Global Policy Institute for helping us in the preparation and running of this stimulating project. We should also like to thank the Office of the European Commission in London, who have contributed financially to the conferences and the production of this collection of essays.

Introduction

Henning Meyer

It is no exaggeration to say that in most European Union (EU) member states Britain's role in the EU is seen as an ambiguous one. Successive British governments have been perceived as blocking the deepening of the Union, dividing member states politically and pursuing British national interest through the supranational institutions without any real concern for the consensus-finding nature of many EU processes. A 'Europe à la carte' approach, where supranational solutions are sought if they naturally fit the government's interest and national resolutions are preferred if this is not the case, has increasingly come to be seen as the British approach to European integration.

The country's history in and towards the Union reinforces this ambiguity too. In his visionary speech in

Zurich in 1946, the Conservative war leader and statesman Winston Churchill called for the creation of a United States of Europe. He asserted that 'the structure of the United States of Europe, if well and truly built, will be such as to make the material strength of a single state less important'. Yet when the European Coal and Steel Community (ECSC) was founded, the Labour government of Clement Attlee decided not to join what would become the embryo of European integration. As the story goes, it was Deputy Prime Minister Herbert Morrison who, tracked down to the Ivy restaurant by officials in need of a decision, dismissed the idea with little thought on the grounds that, 'the Durham miners wouldn't wear it'.

Because Britain was a victor of World War II and continued to claim a leadership role in world affairs based on its imperial history, the appeal to join a community with very much damaged continental states was weak. In contrast to Churchill's vision the strength of the British state was seen – and arguably still is seen – as more important than building a powerful supranational institution. Britain only joined the European Economic Community (EEC) under the Conservative Prime Minister Edward Heath in 1973 after the French President Georges Pompidou changed his predecessor Charles de Gaulle's policy of vetoing British membership.

But is this perception of British exceptionalism really well-founded? Is Britain really the odd man out in Europe? Or has this stereotypical perception and Britain's rocky early history as EEC member clouded the view on the reality of Britain's engagement in the 21st Century European Union? These questions need clarification.

In 2008/2009 the Global Policy Institute at London Metropolitan University and the Federal Trust for Education and Research organised a series of conferences that put these questions to the test. Reviewing crucial policy fields such as energy and climate, the EU's social dimension and immigration as well as examining the politics of the single market, the EU budget and the Lisbon Treaty, the conference series analysed Britain's involvement in the EU in a structured approach. This edited volume brings together some of the most insightful contributions to the conferences and offers an analytical rather than perceptional view of Britain's position with respect to 'mainstream Europe'. Our results are very mixed.

In areas such as the environment, the internal market and foreign policy Britain can be considered part of the European mainstream. On budgetary policy, the British rebate is the only aspect that can be regarded as 'exceptional' compared to other member states. In the particular case of the budget, it looks like the idea of 'juste retour' – the view that the cash return from the EU into a specific member state should be directly related to cash input – is gaining ground in other countries too. At the end of August 2009 for instance, French Prime Minister François Fillon warned that because of strained public finances resulting from the global recession, France's net contributions to the EU were 'coming under pressure'.

In the area of social policy, an area that is still very much nationally dominated, Britain can however be seen as a European exception. Apart from direct instruments such as the European Social Fund (ESF) and the Globalisation

Fund, standard-setting in the single market is one of the main tools of EU social policy. Therefore, the UK's opt-outs from the Charter of Fundamental Rights and the Working Time Directive can be seen as instances where the European menu did not suit the national preferences and Britain therefore rejected the deal. These opt-outs are indicative of Britain's reluctance to develop a more distinct social dimension of the Union. The UK is certainly not the only reluctant member state but this does not make the UK's policy any less removed from the mainstream.

So in terms of involvement in the EU's policy agenda Britain cannot be regarded as an outright exceptional actor. The analysis of different policy fields moreover seems to support the 'Europe à la carte' hypothesis.

But the British societal context, which needs to be seen as backdrop for the more detailed studies in this volume, deserves some brief consideration too. One social aspect that appears to be very strongly developed in the UK, which is less an exception but rather a very pronounced version of experiences that can also be found in other member states, is British public hostility to the workings of the Union that is driven by biased media coverage of EU affairs. Whether the issue is European parliamentary expenses, the real level of the British budgetary contribution to the European Union or staffing levels in the European Commission, British electors seem to receive from their media an often systematically distorted view of the European Union and its workings. The underlying assumptions of much reporting on the European Union in this country, that members of the European Parliament are even greedier in exploiting their expenses than are national MPs, that Britain is uniquely disadvantaged by the structure of a vast and wasteful European budget and that the European Commission is a swollen, corrupt, incompetent bureaucracy – all these are at the very least debatable propositions which are too often presented as obviously true to British audiences. The incessant repetition of these tendentious claims forms a uniquely unpromising background for the public discourse of Britain's future role in the European Union.

This biased media coverage is often paired with a mixing up of policy and polity issues when it comes to the European Union. There is a temptation – again not just in the UK but particularly so here – to declare the totality of the Union's activities unacceptable if the policies coming out of Brussels are not favourable to a certain political analysis. This attitude applies to the left and well as the right of the political spectrum and makes little sense. It is as if the Labour Party were calling for the abolition of the Westminster government, and the exclusive reliance on local government instead, because it did not like the policies of a Tory administration in Westminster.

This difficult societal context makes a facts-based analysis of the British approach to European integration a tricky task. But we think that this volume can make a contribution to clarifying the view on the reality of Britain in the EU and help to structure the way this vital debate is conducted. We have sought to delve beneath the myths and stereotypes rather than to perpetuate them. There is a lot of material in what follows that I believe does precisely that.

Britain and the Single Market

John Cooke

Introduction

It might have been thought, half a century after the establishment of the European Community, and over thirty-five years since UK accession, that it would be easy to take a retrospective view of the UK attitude to particular features of the Community. And in some areas it is relatively straightforward to do so. The UK approach to the Common Commercial Policy or the Common Agricultural Policy, to take two instances, has been relatively consistent. But in other areas – and the Single Market seems to be one of these – it is more difficult to disentangle UK attitudes over more than three decades, and still more difficult to determine whether UK views and policies are actuated by some continuing strand of UK exceptionalism. This chapter seeks to examine some of the issues, ways in which they have changed, and what conclusions can be drawn as to the UK approach to the Single Market. Inevitably, it will have to be selective (debate over the Euro being its biggest omission) but will, it is hoped, throw some light on recurring patterns in UK attitudes.

Concepts of the 'Single Market'

One of the challenges facing any analysis is clarity over the concept of 'the Single Market' itself. A UK reader of the EEC Treaty in 1973, interrogating its provisions for guidance on the UK's accession obligations, would have looked in vain for the terms 'Single Market' or 'Internal Market'. The Treaty refers throughout to 'the common market' or 'the Community'; and treaty obligations (e.g. the 'four freedoms' (free movement of goods, persons, services and capital[1]); agriculture; transport; and Community policies in areas such as competition, state aids and approximation of laws) are set out by reference to their role in the establishment of the common market. In places where 'the Single Market' or 'Internal Market' might have been used (e.g. regarding imported goods entering into free circulation within the Community), terms such as 'a member state' or 'member states' are preferred. The Accession Treaty (1972) follows this pattern. Even so, the 'internal market' was a recognised term in the 1970s[2]. It was only later, in the 1980s and 1990s, that the concept of 'the Single Market' was given a much more definite identity.

Another factor affecting the concept was its broad and undefined ambit. Over its history, the Single Market (under various names) has been an amorphous concept. In Community etymology, its antecedents lay in the coal and steel common market established under Article 4 of the European Coal & Steel Community (ECSC) Treaty (1951) – essentially a market conceived as being industrial goods traded between member states free of customs duties or quotas, discriminatory rules, state aids or restrictive practices. True, the opening Articles of the EEC Treaty (1957) were specific in establishing a common market extending beyond goods to services, highlighted in the concept of the 'four freedoms' (of movement of goods, services, persons and capital) and supported by common policies, rules and approximation of laws. But, arguably, the Treaty provisions of greatest direct impact and ease of implementation were those stipulating free movement of industrial goods within the European Community's Customs Union (achieved in 1968), while those providing for freedom of services and for movement of capital relied more for their implementation on policies and legislative programmes which, it was recognised, required a high degree of harmonisation and would take time to bring into operation. All in all, it is fair to say that the ideas evoked by the terms 'Community', 'common market', and 'internal market' probably began by being predominantly those associated with free movement of goods and people between member states, and only gradually broadened out, in ordinary parlance, to embrace a truly comprehensive single market covering services and capital. In other words, much of the ambit and content of the Commission's Single Market Review of 2007[3] would have been unimaginable (other than as a highly theoretical forecast) half a century earlier.

One aspect of the flexibility of the concept was the continuing variety of views as to the purpose of the 'common', 'internal' or 'single' market. What was it *for*? Article 2 of the EEC Treaty declared that, by establishing a common market and progressively approximating the economic policies of member states, the Community would have as its task 'to promote throughout the Community a harmonious development of economic activities, a continuous and balanced expansion, an increase in stability, an accelerated raising of the standard of living and closer relations between the states belonging to it'. But this left open how the 'common', 'internal' or 'single' market was to be managed in practice. In some sense it was to be a zone of 'Community preference': that had to be the logic of a customs union. But was it to be a 'Fortress Europe', sheltered behind a defensive Common External Tariff and other border barriers? Or was it to be a zone of advanced regional economic integration, but open to the rest of the world? Different member states have taken different views at different times on different aspects of the Community's work; and, with the advance of globalisation, the issue has taken on new meanings. It remains an unresolved question.

The amorphousness of the concept also led to its being prayed in aid as a kind of Janus-like proxy for other ideas. Over the ongoing divide as to whether the Community should be 'broadened' (by new accessions) or 'deepened' (by further integration) hovered a wider agenda encompassing questions as to whether the Single Market was functioning as it should, or whether it needed some change in direction, geographical extent, level of integration, or market ethos. Protagonists on different sides of the argument could – and often did – invoke the Single Market in a variety of ways to bolster their contentions, claiming, on the one hand, that Europe could not be 'broadened' until the Single Market had been satisfactorily 'deepened' or, on the other, that the Single Market was already the subject of sufficient integration and that the 'broadening' of the Community to include new members was now the key priority. Nor was it hard to embrace, Janus-like, both sides of the argument with little apparent inconsistency: at various times there have been those who have contended that the Single Market should be deepened, and the Community broadened, as concurrent processes.

A further factor affecting the concept – or at least the importance attached to various of its aspects – was the trend of developments in the European and global real economy as the twentieth century progressed. In the mid-twentieth century the key characteristic of 'western' and European countries (above all north-west Europe) was their degree of industrialisation and their trade in industrial goods. On the back of this, they had, it is true, established certain globally competitive service sectors. But it was their industrial expansion which was the measure of their economic growth, and their industrial strength that earned them the epithet 'advanced economies', in contrast to the rest of the world, made up of the Eastern Bloc (not necessarily advanced), developing countries, colonies and dependent territories. Against that background, it was natural for the advantages of the 'Community', 'common market', and 'internal market' (as a strong home market base) to be seen mainly in industrial terms: exegeses such as Jean-Jacques Servan-Schreiber's *Le Défi Américain*[4] were explicit in depicting global competition as a world struggle for industrial dominance.

As the twentieth century progressed, all this changed. Even before the UK acceded to the EEC, services had begun to displace manufacturing industry in accounting for the predominant percentage of European employment, as shown in the following table[5]:

	1960	1970	1980	1993	2000	2008
Agriculture	23.8%	16.7%	14.3%	7.1%	4.3%	4.7%
Industry	40.5%	40.5%	35.7%	31.0%	28.9%	26.9%
Services	35.7%	42.9%	50.0%	61.9%	66.8%	68.4%

Many European countries lost their global industrial competitiveness in former staples (e.g. cars, ships, and 'white' consumer goods), retaining a global competitive manufacturing edge only in certain high technology or niche consumer product areas. But they maintained or improved their global competitive position in services, particularly financial services and information technology services. As they did so, they developed economic policies going wider than fostering manufacturing industry. There was a new emphasis on services (as well as a corresponding focus on, for instance, deregulation, the management of environmental change, sustainability, and energy security). Services became a new arena for global competition (matched by the insertion of services into the agenda of WTO multilateral trade negotiations). Inevitably, a corresponding change took place in perceptions of advantages deriving from the 'Community', 'common market', and 'internal market', which were increasingly seen – and challenged – in terms of whether they could provide a crucible for a Community approach to new policies for sustainability as well as a strong home market environment to serve as a base for fostering European businesses in 'new' economic sectors, capable of becoming and remaining globally competitive on a sustainable basis[6].

The Pattern of UK Approaches to the Single Market

How did UK approaches fit into this broad pattern? As with other member states, the UK's approach to the Single Market (or 'Community', 'common market', and 'internal market') was affected by all the conceptual and economic developments identified above. And, like other Member States, the UK attitude was framed, at different times, by domestic political priorities and how sharply these were expressed (notably during the twelve years of the Thatcher government 1979-91). Another factor – as with most Member States – was the degree of confidence in domestic policies and their success. Added to all of these however was a uniquely British element – an ongoing theme of overtly-expressed questioning of the processes and mechanics of European integration through the Single Market. This theme was not necessarily expressed in the terminology of intergovernmentalism versus federalism, but drew on related arguments.

It would not be feasible, in one short chapter, to trace all the twists and turns of UK attitudes to the Single Market over the three and a half decades of UK membership of the Community. This chapter will therefore aim at throwing light on UK approaches at three particular periods: accession (1973), the development of the Single Market concept (1986-93), and the present (2008-09). In doing so, it will focus on UK perceptions of the Single Market as an idea, and the UK's objectives for it, rather than retracing, for instance, all the elements that may have been in play in Intergovernmental Conferences and adaptations to the Treaties, and their effects (actual or potential) on the Single Market.

UK Approaches to the Single Market before and at Accession

There is no doubt that early UK approaches to the Single Market (or 'Community', 'common market', and 'internal market') were much influenced by the perceived need for a broader and more stable market for UK industrial products. In the 1950s, UK policymakers had decided against joining the European Economic Community at its inception. But this had been for broad political reasons, rather than a measured appraisal that Commonwealth economies (where the UK enjoyed tariff preferences deriving from Imperial Preference) would continue to provide an adequate and stable market for the UK's industrial output. In the late 1950s and early 1960s, as UK industrial competitiveness weakened by comparison with that of Germany and the United States, it became increasingly clear that Commonwealth markets could not fulfil this function[7]. The 'old' Commonwealth was gradually withdrawing trade preferences under pressure from other, non-Commonwealth trading partners, and the 'new' Commonwealth markets (typically developing economies) were volatile in their vulnerability to global economic forces (the first to suffer, and the last to recover, from global economic downturns). The European Free Trade Area (EFTA, established at UK instigation in 1960) had allowed some, but insufficient, UK export market growth.

By the later 1960s, it was increasingly apparent that the UK was dependent on European markets for the bulk of its industrial export business; by 1968, about one-fifth[8] of UK industrial exports were to the six EEC members; and while UK exports to EEC had grown by 167% over the period 1958-68, those to the Commonwealth had grown by only 13%[9]. It was noted that the UK average rate of economic growth (GNP per head 1958-67) had been 2.5%, while that of EEC countries had been 4.0%. It was predicted that, if the UK could join the EEC and benefit from tariff- and quota-free market-entry within its customs union, there would be

> the dynamic effects resulting from membership of a much larger and faster growing market. This would open up to our industrial producers substantial opportunities for increasing export sales, while at the same time ex-

> posing them more fully to the competition of European industries. No way has been found of quantifying these dynamic effects but, if British industry responded vigorously to these stimuli, they would be considerable and highly advantageous.[10]

For those involved in the arguments during the period leading to UK accession, this stark contention was one of the most important elements of the case for the UK to join the EEC. Along with references to the Six's economic expansion[11], it remained a telling component of the pro-Europe case during the Referendum campaign in 1975.

It is probably fair to say that this interpretation of the Single Market, rather than any idealistic appeal to its contribution to European integration or ever-closer union, was predominant in UK attitudes in the early 1970s. It was a view based on a traditional understanding of the importance of 'a strong home market' as a basis for wider global industrial competitiveness. This view was not based on any protectionist philosophy: the UK had for long accepted large import volumes (with a consistent negative balance on visible trade, paid for by invisible exports), and the idea of 'Fortress Europe' had few attractions for UK policymakers. Alongside this view was a stated assumption that direct exposure to competition from its European close industrial comparators, undistorted by customs duties or border restrictions, and taking place on the then basis of fixed parities, would be a catalyst for honing UK industrial competitiveness and a spur to investment in UK industry and modernisation of UK industrial relations. This competitive challenge, so it was said, would bring about the progressive industrial transformation that successive UK governments had been unable to achieve.

However – in line with the manufacturing industry-focused orientation that was generally prevalent – little attention appeared to be given to the Single Market's potential for allowing exploitation of service sectors in which the UK could claim to be internationally competitive. Financial services provides an example: although the UK's financial services market in 1972 must have represented a substantial part[12] of the entire financial services market of the EEC's then six member states, little thought[13], appears to have been devoted in the UK to expanding UK financial services across the European market[14]. In part this may have been because many UK financial services businesses were more concerned with Commonwealth and overseas markets than with those of continental Europe. In part it may also have been because UK financial markets, although strong, were subject to a degree of sheltered competition and systems of market-sharing[15]. The relative lack of progress (by 1973) towards harmonisation of the EC financial services framework[16] will also have been a significant factor. And there was widespread realisation in the UK that, whatever the Community's stated aspirations towards a common market embracing free movement of capital, individual member states might harbour contrary ideas, particularly as regards the development of 'national champions' or the maintenance (despite Article 37 of the EEC Treaty) of state trading monopolies. This meant that cross-border mergers between enterprises were not always favoured and could be subject to structural impediments[17].

One other factor in UK attitudes was noteworthy at the time of the accession negotiations and of accession itself. There was a very specific UK approach to common policies and the means by which these should be reflected in Community legislative processes and translated into UK law. It was a matter in which UK lawyers, from the judiciary downwards, took a great deal of interest – perhaps more than lawyers from other Member States. From a legal perspective, there was pronounced discomfort at the notion that any foreign law should prevail over UK law or encroach upon UK jurisdiction[18]. Perhaps this was accentuated by the fact that acceptance of the *acquis communautaire* was particularly challenging for a country whose policymakers had, until then, been accustomed to think of themselves as global standard-setters. The arguments were very fully aired when the European Communities Act – the chosen instrument for giving effect to Community law – was debated in Parliament in 1972. But UK lawyers wished also to ensure, as far as possible, that future Community law would be rendered into UK law by full UK legal processes, avoiding any appearance of the imposition of law from outside the UK. This resulted in a much-stated UK preference[19] for Directives (which aimed at an equivalence of results in practice, after being rendered into the law of member states), rather than Regulations (which were – in theory, at least – 'self-executing' without the need for domestic legislation in member states).

There was, it has to be said, a degree of pure formalism in this approach, obscuring the reality of the change resulting from the UK's participation in a new legal order. It led to some unexpected adverse consequences. First, it avoided confrontation with the sovereignty-sharing inherent in UK membership of the Community, which it might have been healthier to face. Secondly, it sidestepped the substantive question of whether all member states were equally conscientious in their implementation of Community law, leaving the UK authorities relatively unarmed against domestic allegations that, while the UK was rigorous in applying Community law, other member states were not. Thirdly, and perhaps more seriously, it failed to address adequately the question of whether the UK legislature could or should have a role in considering draft European legislation and in determining its attitude towards it. True, Parliament developed a system of 'Parliamentary Scrutiny' to consider proposed Community legislation; but this system has scarcely been rigorous, and sometimes involves Parliament in scrutinising legislation that the Community has already adopted. The system allowed UK governments to implement Community legislation while augmenting ('gold-plating') it with optional added elements deriving from UK government policy rather than Community enactments. In the upshot, it left UK Ministers freer than they might otherwise have been to blame 'Brussels' fairly indiscriminately for unwelcome new elements of regulation, rather than explaining and defending Community obligations and seeking support for them. All these elements – allegations of over-rigorous application of Community law, 'gold-plating', blaming 'Brussels', and the inability of the UK legislature to hold the executive to account in Community matters – were to be recurring themes in the UK's relationship with the Single Market and indeed with the European Community as a whole.

UK Approaches to the Development of the Single Market 1986-93

It is time to fast-forward to a different era, ten years after the UK Referendum, at the high point of the Thatcher administration. Much had, by then, changed in the global economic setting for the Single Market. The GATT Tokyo Round (1973-79) had seen a significant level of global tariff reductions, accompanied by a range of agreements on such topics as government procurement, antidumping, customs valuation, import licensing, subsidies, standards and civil aircraft. By the mid-1980s, major developed countries were planning for the GATT Uruguay Round (1986-94) which was to cover new areas including intellectual property, capital, agriculture and – perhaps above all – services. With these developments came the recognition – in fact if not yet in explicit terminology – that the world economy was 'globalising' and that new Asian players were emerging as rivals to the advanced world as previously defined. Japan in particular was hailed as an exemplary success story, as were Singapore under Lee Kwan Yew and Hong Kong's deregulated and free-trade regime. Servan-Schreiber's polemic setting out requirements for the Community's economic success was succeeded by the more analytical approach taken in Michael Porter's *The Competitive Advantage of Nations* (1990).

All this was a step-change away from the post-war environment into which the Community of Six had been born. It was also a major move forward from the environment in which the UK had joined the Community in 1973. Against the background of new global challenges it was scarcely surprising that there were calls – and not only from the UK – for a fresh approach to what was meant by the Single Market (or 'Community', 'common market', or 'internal market'). Why, when global markets were advancing rapidly, with changes in investment patterns worldwide, should the Community's much-vaunted Single Market be suffering a de facto lack of free trade between its members in significant sectors – both goods and services – of global importance? Was the Community's approach to harmonisation – frequently a search for a precise identity of practice across all member-states – right or practicable? How should the Community plan to compete in a globalising world? Community policymakers and business leaders sought an initiative to accelerate harmonisation and resolve policy discrepancies, so that the Single Market could be a catalyst for growth and innovation, as it had been in the 1960s. The upshot was Delors Commission's push for 'Europe without Frontiers' leading to the Single European Act (SEA, 1986)[20]. This was the first major revision of the EEC Treaty, with an explicit focus on the internal market, setting the Community a seven-year objective of establishing a true Common Market, and codifying European Political Cooperation, the forerunner of the European Union's Common Foreign and Security Policy. In economic terms, its core objective was to create a Single Market within the Community by 1992, a date by which, it was hoped, the necessary legislative reforms could be completed. To facilitate this, the SEA reformed the legislative process by introducing the cooperation procedure and by extending qualified majority voting to new areas. In doing so the SEA was designed to remove remaining barriers between member states, accelerate harmonisation and increase the competitiveness of European countries.

These approaches to reinvigorating the Single Market aroused ambivalent feelings from the UK government. On the one hand, there was much to agree with: the UK authorities were European leaders in pursuing comparable policies with a substantial degree of success. From being, in economic terms, the 'sick man of Europe' of the mid-1970s, the UK had radically shifted position by the late 1980s. Thatcher's government had taken ground-breaking steps towards 'pushing back the frontiers of the state', with initiatives to privatise nationalised industries (both manufacturing and services), a confrontational approach towards breaking the power of the unions, and a conscious policy of promoting 'enterprise', accompanied by economic deregulation. In its privatisation policy for key sectors such as telecommunications and energy utilities the UK was not only breaking with the past but also taking steps that were wholly novel in the Community. In promoting enterprise and deregulation the UK government was benchmarking itself against Community and other global comparators in terms of yardsticks such as ease of doing business or legal processes required for setting up a new enterprise: more widely, the Enterprise & Deregulation Unit set up by Lord Young of Graffham conducted in-depth enquiries into regulation affecting particular sectors (finding, more often than not, that regulatory burdens arose not from EU legislation but from layers of domestic rules and requirements at UK government and local authority level). These measures, begun during Thatcher's first term, were pursued with increasing vigour in her triumphal, post-Falklands War second term. They formed a liberalising background that in many ways might have predisposed the UK authorities towards the SEA, and to work with the grain of efforts to liberalise the Single Market.

But however laudable the liberalisation of the Single Market as an end, there was a good deal of British distrust of the means. Would the legislation envisaged in the SEA result in inward-looking and burdensome new Community encroachments, detracting from the UK victory over the 'Rebate', delivered at the Fontainebleau European Council in June 1984 after pertinacious negotiations with Community partners? Thatcher's appointment of Lord Cockfield – a trusted Thatcherite[21] – as Commissioner in 1984 was one of the great ironies of the history of UK attitudes to the Single Market. Relied upon by her to keep any excesses of the Community

1992 legislative programme under 'realistic' (in her terms) control, he instead followed and built upon the logic of 'Europe without Frontiers', launching his comprehensive White Paper (June 1985). This comprised 300 proposals for legislative action, systematically structured and with a rigid timeline requirement (then unusual in Community programmes) that every proposal had to be accompanied by a target date for adoption within the countdown to December 1992. The measures included a good number incorporating a modernised view of harmonisation, in which mutual recognition, rather than an identity of regimes, was the guiding principle. Although conceived for the benefit of the Community as a whole, these proposals proved to be virtually entirely in line with UK interests and objectives, particularly in the field of financial services[22]. With further irony, the resultant pattern of new legislation was acclaimed in the UK – particularly after Major succeeded Thatcher – as a victory for the UK's vision of the Single Market, and claimed by UK spokesmen within the Community as one of the UK's *communautaire* achievements placing Britain 'at the heart of Europe'.

The Cockfield White Paper did not, in the event, bring about a full liberalisation of the Single Market. Over the years which followed, the UK was quick to point out remaining failings – as were others, including the Commission in its impact report on measures taken since 1986 'The Single Market and Tomorrow's Europe' (1996). This highlighted sectors in which substantial barriers to competition remained, including energy, banking, insurance (differing insurance contract laws), telecommunications (continuing public monopolies) aviation and audio-visual business. It also instanced activities by certain member states which negated the Single Market Programme's liberalising measures (the French Government's approach in this regard was vigorously castigated by Professor Patrick Messerlin[23]). The likelihood of some of these problems was already apparent during the debate on Single Market liberalisation in the late 1980s and early 1990s and discussions on individual Directives. All in all, while the 1992 Programme could be guardedly welcomed, there was ongoing scepticism over its likely results in practice, despite a strong outreach campaign by Lord Young to alert British business to the opportunities – and the competitive challenges – that could result from it.

One core feature of the Single Market debate in the 1980s-90s was, again, the question of intention: what was the Single Market *for*? The debate underwent a watershed year in 1988. The prevailing view in the Commission at that time was that the ultimate aim of the Single Market had to be consistent with the Community's wider objective of open world markets through multilateral trade negotiations. But even the Commission was by no means united in this view: earlier in 1988 EU Trade Commissioner Willy de Clerq had said 'We see no reason why the benefit of our internal market liberalisation should be extended unilaterally to third countries'[24]. Even allowing for 'unilaterally', this was different in spirit from the position taken by Thatcher in her Bruges speech

(September 1988)[25]. The full ambit of the Bruges speech (titled 'Britain & Europe') goes well beyond the confines of this chapter. But its central message set a very clear purpose for the Community, and therefore for the Single Market:

> The Community is not an end in itself. Not is it an institutional device to be constantly modified according to the dictates of some abstract intellectual concept. Nor must it be ossified by endless regulation. The European Community is the practical means by which Europe can ensure the future prosperity and security of its people in a world in which there are many other powerful nations and groups of nations.

She went on to set out her guiding principles (cooperation between sovereign states, encouraging change, openness to enterprise, openness to the world, and Europe and defence). Of these, openness to enterprise and openness to the world were probably the least controversial to her Community hearers and probably set out most of her prescription for the Single Market:

> If Europe is to flourish and create the jobs of the future, enterprise is the key. The basic framework is there: the Treaty of Rome itself was intended as a Charter for Economic Liberty. But that is not how it has always been read still less applied....The aim of a Europe open to enterprise is the moving force behind the creation of the Single European Market by 1992. By getting rid of barriers, by making it possible for companies to operate on a

> Europe-wide scale, we can best compete with the United States, Japan and the other new economic powers emerging in Asia and elsewhere.
>
> And that means action to free markets, action to widen choice, action to reduce government intervention. Our aim should not be more and more detailed regulation from the centre: it should be to deregulate and to remove the constraints on trade.[26]

The Bruges speech was probably the moment that brought into full focus a UK perception – very different from that of the early 1970s – that continental economies no longer provided an example of successful growth for the UK to follow: this was reflected in UK criticisms of the Community and many individual member states as corporatist instruments of dirigisme, sheltered competition and 'Euro-sclerosis'. It was a view consistent with the whole thrust of Thatcher's policies, reflected, for instance, in her insistence that the City of London should be an open international financial centre serving the world, in contrast with the more restricted vision put forward by certain member states for the financial centres in their territories. No doubt it was a view other member states might have rebutted with counter-accusations. But it was perhaps a noteworthy gesture towards some of Thatcher's sentiments that, in the following month, the Commission's statement setting out Community policies was titled 'Europe, World Partner'[27].

This brief overview has not examined all of the aspects (it has not, for instance, covered the UK attitude to the Social Chapter of the Maastricht Treaty or to Schengen), nor dealt with some episodes with important Single Market implications (such as Westland affair in 1986). No doubt successive Conservative governments may have been justified in their sentiment that, if the Single Market's liberalising objectives were to be fulfilled through a genuinely free-market approach, some sharp change of mindset was needed. On the other hand, scepticism over the very foundations of, and justification for, the European project (as instanced in Thatcher's famous 'No, No, No!' speech on 30 October 1990) must have meant that many opportunities for leadership were lost. This scepticism continued to be reflected in a number of ways. One was the way that it became – and largely remains – a matter of UK official practice to give no credit to the Community for any benefits it may have brought, while often resorting to blaming 'Brussels' for unpopular measures. Partly this resulted from the approach at the time of accession (already discussed) to Community policies and how they should be rendered into UK law and practice. But it went deeper, as manifested in other, connected ways. One was the way in which Community support (e.g. funding for some regional project) was rarely if ever publicly acknowledged, as it would be in other member states (Irish national and local bill-boards detailing new road schemes, for instance, make this a feature).

In turn, this raises a question as to whether, over the 1980s and 1990s, the UK became in some ways less well adapted than before to comfortable Community membership. It could be argued that Community membership works best for those member states that have a regional tier of government to which the Community institutions can relate alongside their dealings with central government: the Commission's relationships with the German Länder, or the Italian regions, are examples. But in the UK, particularly at the time of the Thatcher government's confrontations with the Greater London Council, and her attempted curbs on local authorities and restructuring of their finances via the Poll Tax, there was no disposition to countenance – still less encourage – direct dealings between Community institutions and local or regional tiers of government in the UK, and a strong determination to impose central government management on all funding from Community sources. One effect of this was probably a reduction of Community visibility at local level in the UK, restricting perceptions of the Single Market, as regards both acceptance of its benefits and appreciation of the scope for local or regional authorities to deal direct with the Community, as a potential resource.

Whatever these vicissitudes, one key dynamic feature of the Community, predicted by advocates of entry in the early 1970s, had certainly come to pass. It will be remembered that in 1968 about 20% of UK industrial exports went to the six member-states of the then EEC. By 1995, the Community had grown to fifteen member states. Over the same period, the percentage of UK industrial exports to these fifteen countries had steadily grown, as shown in the following table:

Percentage of UK industrial exports to EEC (15)	1970	1975	1980	1985	1990	1995
	40%	42%	52%	54%	58%	58%

This is one measure of the steady integration of the UK into the Community, in economic and commercial terms, over the UK's first two decades of membership.

UK Approaches to the Development of the Single Market Today

It is time to fast-forward again, by more than a decade, to a time at which the challenges faced by the Single Market have again undergone a transformation. In many ways, the early years of the twenty-first century were a period of outstanding success for the Single Market as 'an area without internal frontiers' shared by 27 Member States. Much of what successive UK governments had envisaged for a 'wider', rather than 'deeper', Community had come to pass. Until the financial crisis of late 2007, and in spite of hesitation over some aspects of integration (particularly for energy), implementation of the 'Europe, World Partner' concept appeared to be moving forward. In agriculture, despite enlargement, the Community had sustained a reforming position in the WTO in which it was offering substantial real cuts in agricultural support. In industry, necessary adaptations were gradually taking place (often business-led, in those member states where industrial employment carried high social costs). In services, the Services Directive (2006)[28] had acknowledged that services represented

70% of Community employment (particularly for women) and put in place a system for greater services market openness between member states, particularly for small and medium size enterprise (SME) service-providers, to be implemented by December 2009. For the UK, it was estimated that the implementation of the Directive by all Member States was likely to bring the following benefits:

- Welfare increases of between 0.4% and 0.6% per year, which equates to an increase of £4.1 billion to £6.1 billion per year;
- Increased output by up to 4.2%;
- Prices for services will fall by between 0.3% and 4.6%;
- Increased cross-border trade of up to 6.1%;
- Increased employment opportunities with potentially up to 81,000 jobs being created in the UK.

In all these ways, the Single Market was becoming better adapted – as desired by the UK – to a globalising world in which the Community's comparative and competitive advantage was likelier to be in services rather than in other sectors.

These measures brought undoubted benefits to the Community. According to the UK Department for Business, Innovation & Skills the Single Market has brought benefits of globalisation to both European and UK businesses and consumers, and has helped deliver the Lisbon Agenda goals of growth and jobs. There has been an increase in EU wealth: EU GDP in 2006 was 2.2% higher than it would have been without the Single Market (an average increase in benefits to consumers of €518 per person). EU employment has grown by 1.4% (1992 – 2006) due to the Single Market (an extra 2.75 million jobs across Europe). There has been an increase in foreign direct investment from £16bn in 1992 to £106.5bn in 2006, with the Single Market being a main contributory factor. Over the same period intra-EU trade has increased as a percentage of EU GDP from less than 25% in 1993 to 35% in 2005 and EU external trade has also increased, from 6.9% to 12.3% of EU GDP. Between 2002 and 2007, the average cost for setting up a business in the EU(15) has fallen by over 30% (from €813 to €554) and there has been a reduction in administration burden for firms (from some 24 days to some 12 days). There have also been savings of between 10% and 30% from open and more competitive public procurement rules, increasing the amount of resources available to government and/or improving the quality of government services[29].

These trends represented substantial gains. From the UK point of view, they were particularly marked in the field of financial services, where there were significant advances towards an integrated Single Market. Following discussions under the UK Presidency (1998) the Commission had published its Financial Services Action Plan (1999) suggesting indicative priorities and time-scales for legislative and other measures to tackle three strategic objectives: ensuring a Single Market for wholesale financial services; open and secure retail financial markets; and state-of-the-art prudential rules and supervision. In 2001 work under the FSAP was reviewed in the Lamfalussy Report, which recommended a four-level approach to implementing financial services legislation in certain fields (extended in 2004-05 to all financial services sectors). In parallel, the Commission had established four Expert Groups in 2003 to provide reports on the financial integration of banking, insurance, securities and asset management sectors. Following their reports, Commissioner McCreevy recognised symptoms of 'regulatory fatigue' and published a consultative Green Paper (May 2005) recognising the need to consolidate progress and provide for better transposition and more rigorous enforcement and calling for a debate on supervisory convergence. A White Paper on future policy (November 2005) set further objectives for integrating the Single Market in financial services. Whatever differences of opinion there might be on details, the general direction of travel was very much in line with UK objectives. The Community's approach tended towards recognising the merits of Member States having a single regulator on UK lines[30], and also represented a general acquiescence in the UK view that prudential regulation (based on tests of soundness of providers rather than detailed product- or price-control) should be a key yardstick of good regulation (there was less consensus on the UK contention that regulation should be principles-based and that a certain number of corporate failures among providers was an acceptable price to pay for this).

Had the global economy continued on an even keel from 2007, there would have been much to reassure UK doubters that the Single Market was, in most areas, developing in line with UK preferences. True, there remained considerable leeway to be made up: removal of remaining barriers in the Single Market would, it was thought, lead to a further increase in EU GDP of 2.2%, and the creation of an additional 2.75 million jobs across the Single Market. In addition, there were estimates that full implementation of the Mutual Recognition principle would lead to an increase of 0.18% in EU GDP; greater financial market integration could boost EU GDP by 1.1%; the Single Community Patent could lead to savings of €30,000 per patent; each 5% reduction in trade barriers across the Single Market could produce a 2% increase in EU productivity; and a further 25% reduction in administrative burdens in the EU could boost EU GDP by up to 1.5% (around €150 billion). The prospects for achieving these could moreover be regarded as reasonable, over time. But the global financial crisis changed any such assumptions, reigniting some of the long-running debates on the purpose and management of the Single Market.

This chapter is not the place to discuss all the causes and consequences of the global financial crisis. Suffice it to say that it was a crisis of liquidity, raising issues over the methodology of supervision and radically questioning existing assumptions about the role of certain financial instruments in increasing or reducing financial volatility. Many countries produced analyses of the crisis, its causes, impact and remedies: within the EU, the two most influential texts were probably the de Larosière Report (25 February 2009) and the Turner Review (published by the UK Financial Services Authority (FSA) in March 2009). They showed a substantial degree of agreement that the crisis had challenged assumptions that the market was self-equilibrating: there had been a belief that recent trends in risk management had rendered the market even more resilient and self-equilibrating (the IMF had said so in its Global Stability Report in April 2006), but this belief had been proved wrong. The Turner Review added that, from the UK point of view, there were important issues regarding the 'Single European Passport' system within the Single Market:

> Depositors in one country (or their government) are vulnerable to the failure of banks in another country if the home country concerned lacks the supervisory resources to ensure bank solvency, or the fiscal resources or willingness to fund bank rescue, and if the deposit insurance cover is low and unfunded. The approach to bank branch passporting rights, at least as they apply to branches conducting retail business, therefore requires review...[31]

In other words, said Lord Turner (FSA Chairman), there must be 'either more Europe or less Europe': the Single Market's current arrangements were untenable for the future and must be changed through some combination of:

- more European coordination in regulation, supervision and deposit insurance; and
- more host country national powers in regulating and supervising the branches of banks based in other member states.

In its Communication to the Council of 27 May 2009[32] the Commission broadly accepted this kind of analysis and set out the basic architecture for a new European financial supervisory framework, promising legislative proposals in autumn 2009 to give effect to it, for adoption in time for the new arrangements to in operation during 2010. Its key components would be a European Systemic Risk Board (ESRB) to monitor and assess potential threats to financial stability arising from macro-economic developments ('macro-prudential supervision') and a European System of Financial Supervisors (ESFS) comprising the three existing 'Lamfalussy' Committees of Supervisors, transformed into new European Supervisory Authorities, i.e. a European Banking Authority (EBA), a European Insurance and Occupational Pensions Authority (EIOPA), and a European Securities Authority (ESA).

The detailed aspects of these proposals are beyond the scope of this chapter. But the varying climate of debate surrounding them, both in the UK and in other member states, tended to demonstrate the ongoing durability of UK concerns over the Single Market, and how easily these concerns could be provoked. For many in the UK, there were two key questions concerning the global financial crisis: (1) what response should there be? and (2) who should manage it? Answers clearly needed to be provided: in their absence, the Single Market would not work, if different national supervisors could not trust one another (the gravamen of Lord Turner's strictures). But what should the answers be? Did the Community appreciate the risk of rushing to answer (2) before (1)? It was not clear whether some member states' authorities did, judging by some proposals from continental countries for regulating private equity and hedge funds, which had arguably played little part in the crisis. What importance did the Community accord to financial intermediation as an essential economic activity within the EU? Was the role of the City of London as the Community's *de facto* financial centre valued by Community partners?[33] Would proposals for changing Single Market rules take account of the need for Europe to retain an open financial services market? Or would there be – as spokesmen in some member states appeared to suggest – a reversion to some 'Fortress Europe' approach, under which the Single Market's financial regulatory system would be reformulated as a body of protective rules aimed at excluding 'foreign financial mad cows'[34] from Community markets and at much more detailed regulatory systems focusing on product control, reversing the advances in prudential supervision over the years since the FSAP White Paper? In the UK view, key features for any future Single Market regime for financial services needed to include:

- a positive contribution to regulatory convergence at the global level and to the integrity of the Single Market, rather than any retreat from them;
- market structures that promoted competition and openness to international participants;
- regulation that blended necessary controls with scope for innovation;
- dialogue and transparency between regulatory authorities and market practitioners;

- promotion of easier access to emerging markets and growth in international trade; and
- recognition that the international financial market in the UK was and should remain one of the EU's strategic assets.

Internal EU debate over 2009-10 will reveal how these issues are settled and what changes to the Single Market are made. But the current controversy has highlighted, once again, the potentially wide rifts within the Community on the question: 'What is the Single Market *for*?'

It is probably the debate over future financial regulation in the Single Market that is the most salient issue affecting current UK attitudes. But this should not be allowed to overshadow completely the work undertaken in the Single Market Review (2007)[35] and discussed in the Commission text 'The Single Market Review: One Year On' (2008)[36], and the wider prospects for the Single Market's future. Both noted that a significant number of Single Market improvements were being worked upon and were within reach. This serves to underline that, despite doubts over the best regulatory response to the global financial crisis, there remains much in Single Market developments that is on lines long advocated by the UK. Within the UK itself, other developments – notably devolution and the creation of Scottish and Welsh jurisdictions in addition to Northern Ireland – will also have long term implications for the ways in which the UK and its constituent parts will relate to the Single Market.

Benefits to the UK of the Single Market

Despite the recurring themes of this chapter regarding UK attitudes to the Single Market – the Treaty terms, the amorphousness of the 'Single Market' concept, the ongoing debate as to its purpose and intended degree of openness, its invocation to support sometimes conflicting arguments, and the backcloth provided by the demands of the real economy – there can be little doubt that the Single Market has been of decided benefit to the UK. As regards trade, the latest figures (based on both UK export and import data for 2008) show that 51% of the UK's trade is with the EU, and it is estimated that 3-3.5 million UK jobs are linked both directly and indirectly with the EU. As for investment, half of the foreign direct investment in the UK in 2007 came from the EU (£315bn out of £631bn); the rest of foreign investments made in the UK are often aimed at serving the whole EU market; and the UK Trade & Investment (UKTI) Inward Investment Report for 2007-08 estimates that EU FDI created 14,296 new jobs in the UK (approximately one third of all new jobs created in the UK from inward investment). The investment figures are illustrated by the following chart of direct investment in the UK by area (2007):

EU27	50%
The Americas	32%
Asia	9%
Other Europe	7%
Other	2%

Added to these detailed figures are, naturally, the wider gains which were recognised at the time of accession but are now frequently taken for granted. These include basic Single Market freedoms such as the right to live, study and work across Europe; economies of scale for UK pan-European industries such as auto manufacturing or aerospace; and EU funding for research, which currently outweighs UK contributions. Finally, it is estimated that, if all Lisbon Agenda targets were met, UK wealth could increase by an estimated 7% by 2025 (benefiting every UK person by over £1,500). It has frequently proved difficult, in the heat of an ongoing political debate – in which the UK has often had a degree of right on its side – for these advantages to be assessed objectively. But, as factors in the UK's participation in the Single Market, they remain as real and tangible as when the UK first acceded more than three and a half decades ago.

Notes

1 A 'fifth freedom' – free movement of knowledge – was proposed by the Commission in 2007-08.

2 The OED cites the *Economist* (1 February 1975) as its earliest example of the usage 'the internal market'.

3 COM(2007)724 of 20 November 2007.

4 Published 1967.

5 Source: Eurostat: figures for 1993 are included to illustrate the situation at completion of the Single Market under the Single European Act (1993); the slight rise in the percentage for agriculture in 2008 (the latest year available) reflects the accession of the twelve new member states.

6 Highlighted in the Lisbon Agenda, adopted in 2000 by the European Council, aiming to 'make Europe, by 2010, the most competitive and the most dynamic knowledge-based economy in the world'.

7 Noted in 1961 in John Pinder: *Britain and the Common Market* (London, 1961), p. 114.

8 White Paper *Britain and the European Communities* 1970.

9 White Paper *Britain and the European Communities* 1970.

10 White Paper *Britain and the European Communities* 1970: these dynamic effects were regarded as essentially non-quantifiable. See table on p. 30 for the outturn 1970-1995.

11 '[The common market] offers the best framework for success, the best protection for our standard of living, the best foundation for greater prosperity. All the original six members have found that. They have done well – much better than we have – over the past 15 years…' Referendum campaign leaflet: 'Why you Should Vote Yes' (1975).

12 Comparative statistics are hard to establish across financial services (banking, insurance and securities) as a whole, but insurance may offer a partial proxy: in 1972 the premium income of the UK insurance industry was equivalent to about 31% of the total premium income of the of the EEC's six member states (all in US$ terms), Sources: Sigma No 5 (May 1975) and Assuranz-Compass Yearbook 1978.

13 For instance, the White Paper (1970) confined itself to suggesting in general terms (paragraph 92) that 'the contribution of the City of London should bring benefits not only to the United Kingdom, but to the other members of the EEC as well. The City can offer a wide range of financial and commercial services…which is unrivalled outside the United States. With greater awareness of the diversity and sophistication of these

facilities both we and our future partners can expect to gain increasing advantage.'

14 The City of London had other preoccupations over this period (the end of the Bretton Woods system, the 'Barber Boom' and (from 1974) the secondary banking crisis).

15 A decade before the City of London's 'Big Bang' (1986).

16 The first Directive concerned with insurance (the Reinsurance Directive (Council Directive 64/225/EEC)) had been adopted in 1964; the First EC Banking Directive was adopted in 1977.

17 Such as cross-holdings which effectively stymied takeover bids, whether domestic or foreign.

18 UK officials strongly resisted the Commission's attempts at extraterritorial reach in the Dyestuffs Case (1972) in which Imperial Chemical Industries (ICI) was reportedly implicated.

19 Particularly espoused by Lord Diplock, leading to references to 'le Diplockisme' in European legal debate.

20 Signed in February 1986 on the basis of political agreement reached at the Luxembourg European Council of 3 December 1985. It came into effect on 1 July 1987, under the Delors Commission.

21 Increasingly distrusted by her as he warmed to his European role, particularly after he reminded her that the EEC Treaty mandated the Commission to present proposals for the harmonisation of indirect taxes (quoted in Sir Roy Denman: *The Mandarin's Tale* (London, 2002), p. 213) and so not reappointed.

22 In banking, for instance, the programme covered by the Cockfield White Paper saw the adoption of the Bank Accounts Directive (86/635/EEC), the Capital Liberalisation Directive (88/361/EEC), the Own Fund Directive (89/299/EEC), the Solvency Ratio Directive (implementing Basel I) (89/647/EEC), the Second EC Banking Directive (providing for a 'Single Passport')

(89/646/EEC), the Monitoring and Control of Large Exposures Directive (92/121/EEC), the Capital Adequacy Directives (93/6/EEC and 93/31/EEC) and the Deposit Guarantee Directive (94/191/EEC).

23 See Patrick Messerlin: 'Marché unique des services: encore un effort vers la libéralisation', *Le Monde Economie*, 24 December 1996, commenting on the UK FCO/DTI White Paper *Free Trade & Foreign Policy: A Global Vision* (1996).

24 *Financial Times*, 14 July 1988, quoted in Paola Bongini: *The EU Experience in Financial Services Liberalisation: A Model for the GATS Negotiations* (Louveciennes, Société Universitaire Européenne de Recherches Financières (SUERF), 2003).

25 Speech to the College of Europe, Bruges, 20 September 1988.

26 Mrs Thatcher went on to give chapter and verse in fields which remain relevant today, instancing the openness of the City of London, UK market-opening for telecommunications, air services and coastal shipping, the need for implementation of the Community's commitment to free movement of capital, and for a genuinely free European market in financial services, and highlighting the resultant benefits for European consumers.

27 European Commission, 19 October 1988.

28 Directive 2006/48/EC, to be implemented by December 2009.

29 Source: estimates used by the Department for Business, Innovation and Skills.

30 The UK Financial Services Authority was established under the Financial Services and Markets Act 2001.

31 Turner Review, p. 38.

32 COM (2009) 252 FINAL.

33 For the Commission, President Barroso volunteered a very positive public response to this question at a No 10 Press Conference on 29 June 2009, when he said 'The City of London is

very important for Britain but also for Europe and it is giving a very important contribution for jobs and growth not only here but in Europe.'

34 The author is indebted to Paris Europlace for this graphic phrase.

35 COM (2007) 724 of 20 November 2007.

36 SEC (2008) 3064 of 16 December 2008.

Energy and Climate Change: is the UK an Environmental Champion in Europe?

Peter Luff

Since its accession to the then European Community in 1973, the United Kingdom's dealings with its European partners, and most particularly the Commission, in the sphere of environmental policy have undergone a noticeable evolution. Beginning with both suspicion and an idiosyncratic set of priorities, the UK has, over the years, taken a central and ultimately positive role in both the shaping and the execution of progressive policies in this area, especially on climate change.

This evolution has to be placed in the context of the change that has taken place in environmental priorities over the past 35 years. When the UK first joined the European Community, the concerns of the environmental movement were primarily directed at the dangers of pollution in all its forms, from the effect of the emissions of power stations on forests through to growing concerns over waste disposal, clean water, biodegradable waste and genetically modified crops. It is only in the last two decades that the issue of global warming and climate destabilisation has taken centre stage.

Over that time, the UK's role in Europe has also changed: whereas its early relationship with its European partners was built around a reluctance to allow the Commission to interfere in matters the UK saw primarily as national questions, in time it has moved to being an active partner in setting standards and, indeed, in being at the forefront of moves to limit carbon emissions.

In the 70s and 80s, the UK's approach to tackling environmental issues differed considerably from other member states. It was for a while known as the 'dirty man of Europe' and there were regular protests from Scandinavia over the acid rain falling on Norwegian forests due to the toxic emissions of Didcot's power stations. Unwilling to participate fully in the process of setting Europe-wide environmental standards, British governments resented the imposition of European regulations. Essentially, British governments preferred negotiated agreements with industry over levels of pollution based on general guidelines rather the imposition of internationally negotiated standards. This set it at odds with its European partners and led, on occasions, to conflict. Even Directives aimed at reducing water pollution led to conflict with the Commission and much negotiation before agreement was reached.

The Department of the Environment (DoE), as it was then, not infrequently used the national veto to block or emasculate environmental legislation unwelcome to the UK. The introduction of greater majority voting under the Single European Act and subsequent treaties helped to change the UK's chances of blocking European legislation but it also brought about a change of perspective. Recognising that it could no longer always block unwelcome European environmental legislation, the UK became actively engaged in promoting its own perspective on environmental legislation at a European level and, in recent years, has played a leading role in developing a European perspective on climate change, including setting targets for carbon emission reductions.

Although, in the early days, the British government retreated from playing an active role in building a European response to environmental concerns, the United Kingdom has always had its fair share of both environmental prophets and activists. James Lovelock's 'Gaia' hypothesis played a key role in alerting the world to the immense dangers of global warming caused by anthropogenic activities, most obviously the emission of greenhouse gases. His ideas were taken up by an already lively environmental movement led by key figures such as Sir Jonathan Porritt, Tom Burke, Tony Jupiter and others, who were already actively involved with broader issues of environmental degradation. Organisations such as Friends of the Earth and Greenpeace had attracted active campaigners and were making their presence felt on the world stage. They also received important support from the Prince of Wales, who has frequently strayed into the political arena to make known his passionate views on the environment.

But the person who was able to bring many of these ideas right to the seat of power in this country was Sir Crispin Tickell. A former ambassador to the UN and also a friend of Lovelock, Sir Crispin is credited with having persuaded the then Prime Minister Margaret Thatcher, herself a scientist, to recognise the crucial importance of climate change for the future of the planet.

In a speech to the second climate change conference in Geneva in 1990, she said:

> But the threat to our world comes not only from tyrants and their tanks. It can be more insidious though less visible. The danger of global warming is as yet unseen, but real enough for us to make changes and sacrifices, so that we do not live at the expense of future generations.
>
> Our ability to come together to stop or limit damage to the world's environment will be perhaps the greatest test of how far we can act as a world community. No-one should under-estimate the imagination that will be required, nor the scientific effort, nor the unprecedented co-operation we shall have to show. We shall need statesmanship of a rare order. It's because we know that that we are here today.

If global warming had before 1990 often been seen as one of the issues of the woolly liberal left, it was of great importance that the champion of the free market should have taken the issue on board and, indeed, given support to her Ministers, most especially Environment Minister, John Gummer, in trying to tackle the problem.

Gummer played an important role in bringing environmental issues to the fore in the British context and, during his time as UK Environmental Secretary from 1993-1997 on the European stage. Gummer had long been one the Conservative Party's most pro-European ministers. He played a key role in the 'Convention on Climate Change' meetings held in Berlin and Geneva. The Secretary-General of the United Nations named him as one of a small Committee of Distinguished Persons advising on Habitat II (UN Conference on Human Settlements). In 1996, he was also elected Chairman of the Environmental Committee of the OECD by his fellow ministers. Friends of the Earth called him the best Environment Secretary they had ever had.

When the Labour government took office in 1997, its parliamentary majority – the largest for any party in over a century – raised many expectations among environmentalists that, in addition to other key social issues, environmental dangers and especially climate change would be tackled head on.

Tony Blair had made it quite clear that he saw climate change as a priority for the New Labour government and made it one of the key issues at the Gleneagles European Summit in 2005. By this time, the scientific evidence that linked global warming with carbon emissions was becoming overwhelming and there was a hope that this recognition would be translated into policies commensurate with the scale of the problem.

The Deputy Prime Minister John Prescott was also given responsibility for the Environment and, in that capacity, played a strong and constructive role during the Kyoto negotiations and the following Conference of the Parties (COP) meetings. Indeed, it is claimed that in the small hours of the morning he came very close to persuading the Americans to sign up to the concept of 'contraction and convergence' that was originated by Aubrey Mayer and the Global Commons Institute and was gathering support. However, time and patience ran out. And, of course, it is extremely doubtful that such a radical agreement, had it been made, would have received necessary Congressional ratification. Nevertheless, as in many of the subsequent COP meetings, he and the UK delegation played strong and constructive roles.

Persuading the US and bringing them on board has been one of the central planks of British policy all through the history of global climate negotiations. It is an attitude which has led to great frustration. Throughout the years of the Bush administration, there was a failure to move at the speed necessary to tackle carbon reduction at a global level because of a desire to bring the Americans on board – a hope constantly frustrated at successive meetings of the COP.

Serving as Environment Minister under John Prescott was one of the most radical environmentalists in Britain – Michael Meacher. Totally convinced of the dangers of global warming, Meacher played a major role in trying to push Britain towards a leadership position both in the world and in its own environmental policies. But, like many others with good intentions, his energy and enthusiasm were swept away by the aftermath of the Iraq war, which Meacher opposed. He was also seen as too radical for a British government that was longer on rhetoric than action.

Its prosecution of the Iraq war may well be seen as the event which cost the Labour Party its opportunity to deliver major change in any area, including the environment. Not just the rhetoric of the war but the sheer financial cost and, of course, the greenhouse effect of the war itself, greatly reduced the UK's ability to exercise moral leadership.

Nevertheless subsequent Environment Ministers, and in particular Margaret Beckett, did play key and constructive roles in international negotiations and, indeed, succeeded in shifting the US from outright opposition to at least a willingness to continue talking – a small but important victory in which Beckett's patience in all-night talks played no small part. But that, by itself, did little to implement the immediate tasks that needed to be taken urgently if the worst impacts of global warming were to be averted.

In 2006, David Miliband was moved to the environment brief and quickly went about using green issues to develop a wider policy platform. For Miliband the environment was the 'mass mobilising movement of our age'.

In this brief, Miliband supported the idea of personal carbon-trading schemes – credit cards that form a tally of each person's emissions – which he regarded as going further than the carbon capping scheme run by energy suppliers, and more equitable than tax increases because 'carbon allowances penalise only those that [go] over them'.

Miliband had a strong and informed view of the environment and his brief time at the Department for Food and Rural Affairs brought some hope and his first speeches augured well. He clearly recognised the fundamental importance of climate change but was only to last in that Ministry for 18 months before moving to the Foreign & Commonwealth Office.

The post was filled by Hilary Benn, who, like Miliband, took a pro-active role in both developing European policy and on the global stage. But the demands of a department that had to cope with everything from climate change to animal diseases and farm benefit payments proved too great a range of tasks for effective action and was, under premiership of Gordon Brown, divided into two ministries, one of which, the Department of Energy and Climate Change, was given to Ed Miliband. Miliband has taken over and driven forward a substantial agenda of British and European initiatives in the environmental field. This agenda provides an interesting insight into where the UK stands and where it thinks of itself as standing in the European environmental debate.

UK and Emissions Trading Scheme

Launched in April 2002, three years before the EU's Emissions Trading Scheme (EU ETS), the UK Emissions Trading Scheme was then the world's first economy-wide greenhouse gas emissions trading scheme. This successful experiment,conducted on a temporary and voluntary basis ending in March 2007, is now planned to lead in April 2010 to the set-up of a legally binding climate change and energy saving scheme, the Carbon Reduction Commitment. Aimed at greater energy efficiency and fewer CO2 emissions, the new scheme will put a cap and a price on carbon emissions of around 20,000 UK organisations, complementing the EU ETS and the UK Climate Change Agreements by taking in large non-energy intensive organisations, including large business and public sector organisations. The UK goal for emissions reductions is more ambitious than the European goal, set at the Council in Heiligendamm in June 2007, of 20% committed reductions by 2020, rising to 30% if other countries also make commitments. The UK Climate Change goal is 34% below 1990 levels by 2020 and 80% by 2050. (The EU hopes for 50% reduction by 2050.)

UK and Renewable Energy

At the end of 2007, the UK was using around 5% of renewable energy to produce its electricity. The country is today at the 19th place Europe-wide, behind France (12th) and Germany (14th). The 2003 Energy White Paper stated the objective of 10% of energy to be produced by renewables by 2010 and 20% by 2020, which would match the official European position stated in its climate change and energy package adopted in December 2008, agreed by the UK government. However, interestingly, the more recent official target of the Department for Energy and Climate Change, as stated on its website, is that 15% of the UK energy – electricity, heat and transport – would come from renewable sources by 2020. The recently released UK Low Carbon Transition Plan confirmed this new objective. The Plan also recommends that one third of the electricity generated in the UK should come from renewable sources.

The UK has an enormous potential both in wind energy and wave and tidal energy. However, none of them is fully exploited. Wind energy contributes very little to the total electricity produced in the UK (in 2006, it represented 1% of the total electricity production and 17% of the total renewable sources used for electricity production). Industry in wave and tidal energy is only at its early stage and, although Research and Development is ongoing, no electricity has been produced from it yet.

Hydroelectricity generated in 2006 around 2.1% of UK electricity but further development of the technology is seen in future as uncertain as large scale use is limited because of environmental concerns and lack of terrain and force of rivers. Biomass generated in the UK in 2006 around 2% of total electricity.

The Renewable Transport Fuel Obligation, which entered into force in April 2008, fixes the requirement for British transport fuel suppliers to ensure that 5% of all road vehicle fuel is supplied from renewables by 2010. This could be extended in the near future to all transports. In comparison, the European Renewable Energy Directive states that 10% of the transport energy should be from renewable sources by 2020 and the European Energy and Climate Change Package says that a 10% share of transport fuel consumption should come from sustainable biofuels by 2020.

Various programmes have been established to exploit other available resources – such as solar photovoltaic

(PV), geothermal and micro-generation – but capacity and electricity production are limited in all three cases, especially if compared to other countries such as Germany and Japan for PV. Renewables receive various financial supports, including a billion pounds sterling subsidy per annum by 2010, as stated in the Renewables Obligation, and a tax exemption from the Climate Change Levy. The Office for Renewable Energy Deployment was launched in July 2009 through the Renewable Energy Strategy in order to make sure renewables are delivered and deployed in the UK to achieve the 2020 target.

UK and CCS

The UK moved slowly into Carbon Capture and Storage (CCS), compared to other European countries. Germany set up in September 2008 the world's first complete demonstration of CCS technology, the Schwarze Pumpe pilot. The UK showed early interest in the technology and the potential of CCS in 2006 when the government launched a competition to fund the construction of a 400MW commercial scale CCS power plant in the country to go on line in 2014. After a consultation into how to implement the technology, the government confirmed that any new combustion power station at or over 300 MWe would have to be built with CCS facilities. In June 2009, a proposed Energy Bill was included in the Draft Legislative Programme for the Fifth Parliamentary session 2009-2010, which introduces financial incentives to support up to four CCS demonstration projects. The Low Carbon Transition Plan, released a month later, confirmed this new objective. At the European level, the EU has plans for 12 demonstration plants running by 2015.

Although CCS has recently received strong support from Ed Miliband, the decision to go ahead with the Kingsnorth coal-fired power station before CCS can be implemented has caused fury among environmental campaigners and has severely damaged the government's environmental credentials.

UK Climate Change Act

The UK has been among the first countries of the world to introduce and adopt a long term and legally binding climate change strategy. The UK Climate Change Bill was introduced in Parliament in November 2007 and came into force on 26 November 2008. The official GHG emissions reduction target is now at least 34% by 2020 and 80% by 2050 (below 1990 levels). In comparison, the official EU target, as stated in the EU Climate and Energy Package, is 20% reduction by 2020 (30% if an international agreement is found) and at least 50% by 2050, below 1990 levels. Other key measures in the Act are:

- A carbon budgeting system, through five-year periods, has been set up to set out the trajectory to 2050. Three successive carbon budgets will be set at a time to ensure predictability and flexibility;
- A Committee on Climate Change, under the chairmanship of Lord Turner, acting as an independent and expert body advising the government

on the level of carbon budgets and cost-effective savings, in order to reach the 2050 target. The Committee will submit annual reports to Parliament on the progress achieved and will advise the government on the relevance of including international aviation and shipping emissions into the Act, on adaptation (through an adaptation sub-committee), and on the use of international credits;
- The government must report at least every five years on adaptation, risks, and necessary responses;
- The creation of a Community Energy Savings Programme.

The Act and its targets put the UK in the forefront of the European response to climate change.

Conclusions

How effective has a Labour government been, under the leadership of Blair and Brown, in helping to forge a European environmental policy? In Blair's case, a general enthusiasm and understanding of the crucial effect global warming will have on the environment was dissipated by a range of other enthusiasms and a desire to remain close to the US Administration even during its greatest follies. For Brown, a general lack of Euro-enthusiasm and the sense that climate change is not really his area of interest has, surprisingly, not prevented his government from playing a generally positive role in shaping European and global environmental policy, though this is offset to some extent by a desire to placate business interests when they come into conflict with tackling climate change. Indeed decisions such as the building of a new coal fired power station in Kent before the installation of carbon capture and storage and the commitment to a new runway at Heathrow have lost the Labour Party the support of at least some environmental activists on whose support it will have been counting at the time of the next general election.

It is fair to say that, over the past three decades, the UK has moved from a reluctant partner to one of the driving forces behind the EU's prominent role in tackling global environmental issues. This has been one of the rare occasions in which parts of the media have played an important and vanguard role in taking up the issue of global warming and creating sufficient public support for action to enable the government to act. Certain papers, notably *The Independent*, *The Financial Times* and *The Guardian* made sure that the dangers of climate change received regular and, at times, dramatic coverage and the BBC has also moved from a position of 'balance' to accepting the need to explain and educate rather than merely discuss the issue. During his time as Prime Minister, Blair may have failed to make action match his rhetoric but, at least, he ensured that climate change was high on the agenda of the G8 plus 5 meeting he chaired.

From blocking early Commission initiatives, the UK moved to being a proponent of concerted EU action to tackle climate change and the creation of the Department for Energy and Climate Change headed by a Secretary of State, with a cabinet seat, has both focussed activity and moved it higher on the policy agenda for government. In COP meetings, the UK has frequently played a strong diplomatic role – partly in an attempt to keep the US on board and partly because it has used its relations with both the EU and the Commonwealth to build bridges. Whether it will be able to influence the Copenhagen Summit remains to be seen. The Obama administration, though infinitely more aware of the issues than its predecessor and determined that the US must take action, is nevertheless still handicapped by a far less determined Congress, the vested interests of a massive oil lobby, a religious right and much media ignorance. It has also made it clear that it will pay more attention to a concerted European policy than to that of the UK alone.

The UK also has the opportunity to help the EU build bridges with the developing world and most especially with the fast emerging economies of India and China. Many unofficial links have already been established through non-governmental routes to find new and imaginative methods of cooperation. The UK could play a vital role in promoting these initiatives as part of a new dynamic in European Foreign & Security Policy. But that may have to wait until the final ratification of the Lisbon Treaty.

EU Asylum Policy: Britain on the Margins

Nadine El-Enany and Eiko Thielemann

Introduction

EU law is having an increasing impact on asylum policy in Europe. Member States have gradually pooled policy-making competencies in this area in order better to control asylum flows and to share more equitably responsibilities arising from such migratory movements. For many years, the UK was an active promoter of EU initiatives in this area, as intergovernmental cooperation was seen by British policy-makers as a way to deal more effectively with perceived abuses of the asylum system and EU law was seen as an avenue through which restrictive policy measures could be introduced into national legislation without much domestic opposition. Gradually, however, European asylum policy making has in recent years become less intergovernmental and increasingly influenced by EU institutions. At the same time the focus of EU legal developments has shifted from an exclusive concern about controlling asylum flows towards the setting of European-wide minimum standards for the treatment of asylum seekers and refugees. While the UK had very actively participated in the earlier phase of European asylum cooperation, more recently the government's willingness to cooperate with the other Member States in this area has become more selective, giving rise to claims of British exceptionalism.

Asylum Trends in Europe

During the 1990s there was a great deal of talk about the asylum crisis as the number of asylum applications reached record highs. Many saw this as a new trend that was likely to stay with us, due to changes such as the fall of the Iron Curtain, lower costs of transportations, an expanding global market in human smuggling, etc. While these factors without any doubt have had some impact on migration flows, a look at asylum statistics over the last two decades shows that high asylum numbers in Europe have mostly been driven by particular crises, refugee-producing conflicts such as the Bosnian war in the early 1990s, or the wars in Kosovo, Afghanistan and Iraq at the turn of the century.

The perception among large parts of the general public in the UK and elsewhere, however, has been quite different. *The Sun* reflected popular sentiment about the perceived abuse of the asylum system in one of its headlines: 'Our land is being swamped by a flood of fiddlers stretching our resources – and our patience –

to breaking point'.[1] In a 2003 YouGov poll commissioned by *The Sun*,[2] people in Britain were asked to choose what they regarded as the most important political issue for the UK. The highest number of respondents (39 percent) chose 'immigration and asylum seekers'. In the same survey, 80 percent of respondents agreed with the statement that 'the problem of asylum-seekers is out of control'.

Many in Britain have been convinced that the UK has been the country most affected by this 'asylum problem' as compared with other European countries, believing it to be a particularly popular destination country for refugees and one that consequently has suffered uniquely high 'asylum burdens'. This belief, however, is not borne out in the official statistics.

When comparing Britain with France, the two being quite similar destination countries (in terms of size, wealth, colonial history), we see that the UK was a more popular destination country than France for the ten-year period of 1994 to 2004, but had less of the responsibility share than France in the 1980s as well as more recently. However, even during the high points of UK arrivals in 2000 and 2002, when the UK processed about 100,000 asylum applications annually, numbers were still modest compared to applicants arriving elsewhere. Such as in Germany where more than 420,000 asylum requests were received in 1991, amounting to two thirds of all asylum applications registered in the EU that year. Hence the UK's responsibilities for asylum seekers are not as unique as has sometimes been claimed. Significant variations in asylum applications and the risk of high 'asylum burdens' in the context of increased mobility have led European states, including the UK, to turn to the European level in order to find more effective ways to regulate the flow of asylum seekers and illegal migrants.

National and EU Policy Responses

The economic crisis of the 1970s had made it difficult for European states to be able to absorb the number of immigrants they had been encouraging in previous decades. The closing of legal immigration routes led to a rise in the number of asylum applications which became the only route of entry to Western European countries. As a result, pressure on national asylum regimes was building with the outcome of 'an almost total paralysis of European asylum systems by the beginning of the 90s' (Boccardi, 2002; 27-8). These difficulties led to the growing awareness amongst some European states for the need for an international approach to the problem of asylum. As Boccardi writes, 'in the face of ever increasing cross-border refugee mobility it gradually became apparent that purely national asylum strategies would inevitably be doomed to failure' (2002; 28).

Intergovernmental cooperation on asylum in the form of ad hoc groups began with the Trevi group, established in 1976 by the 12 EC Member States. Its task was to counter terrorism as well as to coordinate policing and other border-control related tasks within the EC. The UK government was a keen supporter of and participant in the work of the Trevi group (Bunyan, 1997; 21). Bigo has written that traditionally the UK has attempted to 'paralyse certain groups at the European Community level, not so much because they are against Europe, but because they are opposed to supranationality and federalism. On the other hand, they have firmly supported intergovernmental bodies including Trevi' (Bigo, 1994; 170). Its intergovernmental nature made it an attractive forum for agreeing policy. According to evidence submitted to the Home Affairs Select Committee, Trevi's particular strength lies in the informal, spontaneous and practical character of its negotiations (Home Affairs Select Committee 1990; 5).

In 1986, the UK Presidency organised a meeting in London in view of working towards the implementation of further compensatory security measures in this area. Member States were represented at this meeting by their Ministers of Interior and Justice Ministers. They resolved to set up an Ad Hoc Immigration Group. It was established on the initiative of the UK with the aim of ending abuses of the asylum process (Webber, 1993; 141). Amongst the areas comprising the work of the Ad Hoc Group was visa policy. At a meeting of the Group in April 1987, a year after its establishment, visa policy was considered as playing a 'particularly important role...in the strengthening of controls at external borders'.[3]

The Ad Hoc Group continued to be active throughout the 1980s and 1990s. In 1990 it produced a draft of the Dublin Convention, which was signed by all Member States in 1990.[4] The UK was one of the first Member States to ratify the Convention. Its content was 'lifted wholesale' from Chapter 7 of the Schengen Agreement entitled 'responsibility for processing applications for asylum', which was signed at the same time as Dublin

(Webber, 1993; 142). The Convention was designed to ensure asylum applicants only made one such claim in Europe, while also preventing asylum seekers from being able to choose the country in which they made their claim by requiring that the individual's claim be heard in the first European Member State through which she passes, i.e. the 'safe third country' notion. A 'safe third country' is one through which an individual has passed and *could have* found protection, but has not done so, either because she did not lodge a claim, or her claim was rejected. Where the individual subsequently travels to another State, she is liable to be returned, subject to the existence of a readmission agreement. The 'safe third country' concept was born out of a conviction that the unequal spread of asylum seekers across the EU was due to 'forum shopping' by applicants, who were perceived as making their way to States in which they believed their claims were likely to be treated sympathetically. The Dublin Convention thus established the rules for the determination of the Member State responsible for hearing the claims of asylum seekers, and is founded on the notion that this responsibility lies with the first Member State with which the asylum applicant establishes contact, whether by the issue of a transit visa, the legal presence of a close family member, or in the absence of these, the first physical contact with the territory (4 June 1985 [1985] OJ L 176; see Lavenex, 1998; 130). State Parties are required to readmit individuals transferred on the basis of the Dublin regime, whilst respecting the principle of mutual recognition with regard to the application of its rules.

Despite the adoption of the Dublin Convention, the relative distribution of asylum seekers across Europe has remained volatile over the years, exemplified by the rapid rise of applications in the UK in the late 1990s. Increasingly, differences in the relative restrictiveness of countries' national asylum regimes have come to be regarded as one of the main reasons for disparities in asylum burdens. According to this view, host countries with a high relative number of applications will try to make their asylum policies more restrictive and other host countries will, as a result, become more attractive destination countries. This has sparked a heated debate about whether countries in which asylum applications have increased in recent years represent a 'soft touch' for asylum seekers and economic migrants using the asylum route of entry. It has also raised concerns that European countries, afraid of being seen as a 'soft touch', have become engaged in the competitive downgrading of refugee protection standards. In order to achieve a more stable and equitable distribution of asylum burdens and prevent a 'race to the bottom' in protection standards, policy makers in Europe have turned to policy harmonisation at the European level. Policy convergence in the field of asylum is seen as the key towards more equitable burden-sharing and an end to regulatory competition.

Moves towards the Common European Asylum System (CEAS) therefore have aimed at establishing a common asylum procedure and a uniform protection status applicable throughout the European Union. These objectives were defined first in the Tampere Programme in 1999 and then confirmed and elaborated in the Hague Programme of 2004. Three main legislative instruments have been adopted. These comprise Directive 2003/9 laying down minimum standards for the *reception* of asylum seekers (OJ L 31, 6.2.2003; 18), Directive 2004/83 on minimum standards for the *qualification* of persons as refugees or those in need of subsidiary protection (Council Directive 2004/83/EC of 29 April 2004 on minimum standards for the qualification and status of third country nationals or stateless persons as refugees or as persons who otherwise need international protection and the content of the protection granted (OJ L 304, 30.9.2004; 12)) and Directive 2005/85 on minimum standards on *procedures* in Member States for granting and withdrawing refugee status (O J L 326, 13.12.2005; 13).

The Impact of the EU on National Policies

There is a widely held view that these developments in European cooperation and early moves towards a common EU asylum policy in particular have had a restrictive impact on asylum policy in Europe, making it increasingly difficult for asylum seekers to reach European territory and benefit from effective protection. This has become known as the 'Fortress Europe' thesis (Geddes 2000; Luedtke 2009). This thesis argues on a theoretical level that Member State cooperation on asylum and refugee matters has fostered restrictiveness through processes of 'venue shopping' (Guiraudon 2000), 'securitisation' (Huysmans 2000) and the legitimisation of 'lowest common denominator standards' (Lavenex 2001). Cooperation, however, does not have to lead to restrictive outcomes. It can also have a 'rights-enhancing' impact on domestic asylum legislation as it curtails regulatory competition and in doing so halts the race to the bottom in protection standards in the EU. Rather than leading to policy harmonisation at the 'lowest common denominator', EU asylum laws can lead to an upgrading of domestic asylum laws, strengthening protection standards for groups of forced migrants. Ultimately, the question of the impact of European cooperation on asylum and refugee policy is an empirical one. Through an analysis of the three main EU asylum instruments in this area, it can be demonstrated how European cooperation has strengthened some refugee rights in the Member States.

The Reception Directive

Traditionally, 'states have strong reservations about granting important rights to asylum seekers because no final decision has been taken yet on the substantive issue of their application' (Lambert, 1995; 103). Nevertheless, the Tampere Conclusions of 1999 provided that the Common European Asylum System should include the establishment of common minimum standards of reception conditions for asylum seekers (Tampere Presidency Conclusions, October 1999). Although this directive has been strongly criticized for not providing adequate standards for asylum seekers (UNHCR 2003), there is little evidence to suggest that the Directive has led to further restrictions of existing national standards.[5] On the contrary, it is shown below that key elements of the Reception Directive have triggered a process that can be expected to lead to an upgrading of domestic standards in several Member States. An analysis of the Directive by the Odysseus Network suggests that EU law on reception conditions does not reflect the lowest common denominator of standards that previously existed in the Member States. The Odysseus Network has noted that the Reception Directive has 'led to the adoption of more favourable provisions at national level than the ones applicable before its adoption in 10 Member States' (Odysseus Academic Network, 2006, 11). The study held that in several Member States the Directive has enhanced protection standards in areas such as provisions for unaccompanied minors, access to health care and access to the labour market. Regarding labour market access, asylum seekers have been given the opportunity to work (after a twelve months waiting period) in countries such as Estonia, France, Latvia, Poland and Slovakia which had previously barred asylum seekers from entering their labour market until a decision on their application for refugee status had been taken (Odysseus Academic Network, 2006, 113). The Odysseus study concluded that the Directive generally did not have the effect of lowering previously higher national standards as would have been possible in the absence of a standstill clause. Possible exceptions noted were Austria and in the United Kingdom where the report states that 'elements of a (potentially) restrictive nature have been introduced'. These consist of limitations on access to employment in Austria and harsher penalties in the UK (Odysseus Academic Network, 2006, 114). Overall the Odysseus Network report held that 'the positive effects of its transposition overshadow its negative effects' (Odysseus Academic Network, 2006, 114).

The Qualification Directive

The Qualifications Directive sets out the rules and principles to be applied by Member States in their identification of refugees and those deserving of subsidiary protection status, and entered into force on 20 October 2004. Critiques of the Directive have highlighted a number of elements of the Directive which have been seen as having the potential to undermine existing protection standards (UNHCR 2007). Despite these criticisms, the assessment of the impact of the Qualifications Directive has in parts been very positive. The introduction of more detailed rules of evidentiary assessment and a clearer definition of persecution have been widely welcomed. Transposition also significantly advanced standards in some Member States where non-state actors of persecution were recognised for the first time, or subsidiary protection was introduced as a concept (Elena 2008; 5). The Directive's provisions on subsidiary protection have been welcomed (UNHCR 2007; 11) as representing the first supranational legislation in Europe defining qualification for subsidiary protection, and creating an obligation to grant this status to those who qualify. Many EU Member States had pre-existing national provisions to afford individuals some form of complementary protection status. The Directive has also been praised for recognising the fact that persons fleeing the indiscriminate effects of violence associated with armed conflict, but who do not fulfil the criteria of the 1951 Convention, nevertheless require international protection (UNHCR 2007; 81). As regards non-state persecution, according to the UNHCR, 'the Qualification Directive has resulted in much greater conformity of legal interpretation on non-State actors of persecution or serious harm [...]. The shift to a focus on the availability of protection, rather than the actor of persecution or serious harm, should be commended. In France and Germany, the Directive has enlarged the scope of grounds for granting protection and thereby reinforced the protection system.' (UNHCR 2007; 9) In Germany, the introduction of the concept of non-State actors of persecution is widely seen as having enlarged the scope of protection. This is reflected in the sharp rise in decisions by the authorities granting refugee status to Somalis since this provision has entered into force under German law (UNHCR 2007; 46).

The Procedures Directive

The Procedures Directive was formally adopted on the 1 December 2005. The key elements that fall under the topic of asylum procedures include the question of access to procedures, procedural guarantees such as the opportunity to communicate with the relevant authorities, access to an appeal process as well as the procedure for the withdrawal of refugee status. The Directive faced calls for withdrawal (ECRE *et al.*, 2004), as well as general criticism from the UN High Commissioner for Refugees strongly (UNHCR, 2004) and from within the EU institutions (European Parliament, 2000). However, the

Directive can be seen to have improved standards of protection for individuals accessing EU territory. The 'safe third country' provisions in the Directive can be seen as having undergone rights-enhancement during the negotiations on the Directive. As Doede Ackers reports, 'There were drafting sessions which resulted in considerably improving the text on rules with respect to the individual consideration in safe third country cases'. (Ackers; 2005, 30). The Commission has stated that the first instance procedures are fully in accordance with the essential rights provided for in Section 192 of the UNHCR Handbook on procedures and criteria for determining refugee status (1979) (Ackers; 2005, 32). What is more, on appeal, the provisions it includes on judicial scrutiny go beyond the Handbook in requiring Member States to ensure an effective remedy before a court or tribunal as opposed to merely 'a formal reconsideration of the decision, either to the same or to a different authority, whether administrative or judicial, according to the prevailing system' (UNHCR Handbook 1979). Further, in a report published by the Refugee Council in 2007 on the UK's implementation of the Procedures Directive, the Refugee Council makes clear that the standards of the Directive would require an improvement of standards in the UK. Article 8(1) for example, states that 'Member States shall ensure that applications for asylum are neither rejected nor excluded from examination on the sole ground that they have not been made as soon as possible' (Refugee Council 2007; 7).

The analysis of the three main EU asylum directives suggests that European cooperation and the development of the common asylum law on the basis of EU minimum standards in this area has curtailed regulatory competition and in doing so it has largely halted the race to the bottom in protection standards in the EU. In more recent years, rather than leading to policy harmonisation at the 'lowest common denominator', EU asylum law has increasingly led to an upgrading of domestic asylum laws in several Member States, strengthening protection standards for forced migrants. While there currently remain significant variations in Member States' implementation of EU asylum law, we expect that the ongoing 'communitarisation' of asylum policy will help to converge Member States' implementation records of EU asylum law and further strengthen refugee protection outcomes in Europe.

Return to British Exceptionalism?

While the UK has cooperated closely on asylum and refugee policy with the other EU Member States for many years, more recent British policy suggests that we have entered a new period. In a Protocol to the 1999 Treaty of Amsterdam, the UK, Ireland and Denmark secured opt-outs from EU treaty provisions on immigration, asylum and civil law. The British and Irish opt-outs allow for the countries to choose whether or not to participate in the discussions on legislation in this area. However, the Protocol gives both countries the right to 'opt into' legislation in these areas at any point should they decide to do so. In practice until recently, the UK has opted out of nearly all proposals concerning visas, borders, and legal migration, but has opted into to all proposals concerning asylum and civil law and nearly all proposals concerning illegal migration.[6] Tony Blair, in an interview on 25 October 2004 described the UK's position as follows:

> With the Treaty of Amsterdam seven years ago, we secured the absolute right to opt in to any of the asylum and immigration provisions we wanted to in Europe. Unless we opt in, we are not affected by it. And what this actually gives us is the best of both worlds.[7]

Recently, however, after years of regular 'opt-ins', the approach of the UK and Ireland has changed and their participation in common policies on illegal migration and asylum policy has become more selective, something criticized by former Justice and Home Affairs Commissioner Vitorino, who has argued that opt-outs in this area 'undermine burden-sharing'.[8] In 2008, the UK (and Ireland) decided not to 'opt into' the EU Return Directive which sets minimum standards for the Member States to follow when adopting policies for the involuntary return (deportation) of illegal immigrants and failed asylum seekers. The British government was:

> not persuaded that this Directive delivers the strong returns regime that the EU needs and that's why the UK government has chosen to exercise its right not to participate in this proposal'. The UK government claimed 'that the Directive makes returning illegally staying third country nationals actually more difficult and more bureaucratic – by introducing restrictions on detention, obligations to

> provide legal aid to irregular migrants, and increasing the possibilities for challenging the return decision.[9]

In other words, the UK felt that the introduction of EU minimum standards would undermine its highly restrictive deterrence policy on involuntary return, in particular domestic laws which allow for the indefinite detention of asylum seekers and illegal immigrants. It means that the UK is now unique in Europe in insisting on the upholding of policies that allow for indefinite detention while other EU Member States who also had domestic policies of indefinite detention, have now agreed to be to be bound by the minimum standards set out by the Return Directive.

Similarly, the UK government has recently stated that it will not not 'opt into' the changes proposed in the new EU Reception Directive (Reception II), which will establish higher common reception standards for asylum seekers across the EU, including giving them greater access to the labour market (after 6 months). The government claims that the Directive would make the UK too attractive to asylum seekers and encourage bogus claims. It also argues that by not opting-in to the new Directive the UK will automatically cease to be governed by any previous EU legislation on reception conditions (Reception I). In other words, the government has not only decided that it considers the Reception II Directive too liberal, it also sees its opt-out of the new Directive as an opportunity to reverse its policy on Reception I. It is a position that has not only been criticized by human rights organizations, but also in a recent report by the House of

Lords (House of Lords 2009). The House of Lord's EU Sub-Committee on Home Affairs argues that there is real uncertainty as to what the UK's legal position will be following the adoption of the new Directive by other Member States. The Committee states that as the UK has opted in to the previous measure but refused to do so for this [new] Directive, it is very possible that the UK will continue to be bound by the previous unamended legislation even though that is not what the government wants. The report states: 'there is no policy or operational reason why the Directive should not continue to operate in the UK in its unamended form.' Commenting Lord Jopling, Chairman of the House of Lords EU Sub-Committee on Home Affairs, said: 'The current situation with the UK's opt-ins on EU home affairs legislation is a recipe for confusion'. It is also a policy which makes it clear that the government has decided to be the only major country in the EU which refuses to be bound by EU minimum standards for asylum seekers, a position that, as we have argued above, cannot be justified on the basis of the assertion that the UK is exceptional in the asylum pressures it faces.

Conclusion

In recent years, asylum policy has increasingly been regulated at the European level, where initial intergovernmental cooperation has evolved into highly 'communitarised' policy making, with EU institutions playing an increasingly important role and Member States being able to take decisions by Qualified Majority Vote. As a result of this process, European cooperation is no longer a mechanism where EU policy is determined by the most restrictively minded Member State. Instead, European cooperation has increasingly put pressure on Member States to fall in line with certain EU minimum standards, which in several cases has meant that Member States have had to change their domestic legislation and grant new rights to asylum-seekers and refugees. The UK, as one of the countries which has come under pressure to 'upgrade' domestic legislation to fall in line with EU standards, has become more reluctant to adopt new EU legislation and more willing to use its 'opt out', allowing the Home Office to side-step the rights-enhancing impact of EU policy in this area. While the UK's 'asylum burdens' are hardly exceptional in comparison to the rest of Europe, the government's decision to deny EU minimum standards of protection to asylum seekers in Britain is.

Notes

1 *The Sun*, 9 March 2000.

2 YouGov survey on Immigration and Asylum for *The Sun* conducted between 11 and 14 August 2003, available at www.YouGov.com.

3 'Declaration of the Belgian Presidency: Meeting of Justice and Interior Ministers of the European Community' (Brussels, 28 April 1987) (Trevi Group – 'ad hoc' meeting on immigration), paragraph a.

4 OJ C254/1.

5 And Article 4 of the Directive explicitly allows Member States 'to introduce or retain more favourable domestic provisions'.

6 The Irish practice has been almost identical to that of the UK.

7 Nigel Morris and Stephen Castle, 'Government pledges to opt out of common EU asylum system', *The Independent*, 26 October 2004
8 Ibid.
9 EP Press release, 'Parliament adopts directive on return of illegal immigrants, Immigration' – 18 June 2008

References

Ackers D. (2005) 'The Negotiations on the Asylum Procedures Directive', *European Journal of Migration and Law* 7.

Bigo, D. (1994) 'The European Internal Security Field: Stakes and Rivalries in a Newly Developing Area of Police Intervention' in Anderson, M. and Den Boer, M. (eds) *Policing Across National Boundaries* (Pinter Publishers, London – New York, 1994).

Boccardi, I. (2002) *Europe and Refugees: Towards an EU Asylum Policy* (Kluwer Law International, The Hague, 2002).

Bunyan, T. (ed.) (1997) *Key Texts on Justice and Home Affairs in the European Union Vol. 1 (1976-1993)* (Statewatch).

ECRE *et al.* (2004) ILGA Europe, Amnesty International, Pac Christi International, Quaker Council for European Affairs, Human Rights Watch, CARITAS-Europe, Médecins Sans Frontières, Churches' Commission for Migrants, Save the Children in Europe, Call for withdrawal of the Asylum Procedures Directive (22 March 2004).

ELENA (2008) The Impact of the EU Qualification Directive on International Protection, Report by the European Legal Network on Asylum.

Geddes, A. *Immigration and European Integration: Towards Fortress Europe?* (Manchester University Press, Manchester and New York, 2000).

Guiraudon, V. (2000) 'European Integration and Migration Policy: Vertical Policy-making as Venue Shopping', *Journal of Common Market Studies*, Volume 38 Issue 2, pp. 251–271.

Home Affairs Select Committee (1990) *Practical Police Cooperation in the European Community*, HC 363-I, 5 (London, HMSO).

House of Lords (2009) Press Release, 'Opt-Out from asylum reception conditions directive will highlight recipe for confusion over EU opt-ins', pn240309euf, Tuesday 24 March 2009 http://www.parliament.uk/parliamentary_committees/lords_press_notices/pn240309euf.cfm

Huysmans, J. (2000) 'The European Union and the Securitization of Migration', *Journal of Common Market Studies*, Vol 38, No 5, pp. 751-757.

Lambert, H. (1995) *Seeking Asylum: Comparative Law and Practice in Selected European Countries* (Martinus Nijhoff, Dordrecht, 1995).

Lavenex, S. (1998) '"Passing the Buck": European Union Refugee Policies towards Central and Eastern Europe', *Journal of Refugee Studies*, 11, 2, p. 130

Luedtke, Adam (2009) 'Fortifying Fortress Europe? The Effects of September 11 on EU Immigration Policy', in Freeman, G. and T. Givens (eds) *Immigration after 9/11*, New York, Palgrave, pp. 127-46.

Odysseus Academic Network (2006) 'Comparative overview of the implementation of the Directive 2003/9 of 27 January 2003 laying down minimum standards for the reception of asylum seekers in the EU Member States'.

Refugee Council (2007) 'Refugee Council response to UK Implementation of Council Directive 2005/85/EC of 1 December 2005 laying down minimum standards on procedures in Member States for granting and withdrawing refugee status' (Refugee Council, October 2007).

UNHCR (2003) 'UNHCR annotated comments on Council Directive 2003/9/EC of 27 January 2003 laying down minimum standards for the reception of asylum seekers' (July 2003).

UNHCR (2004) Press Release, Lubbers calls for EU asylum laws not to contravene international law (29 March 2004).

UNHCR (2007) 'Asylum in the European Union: A Study of the Implementation of the Qualification Directive', November 2007. (Brussels, UNHCR).

UNHCR Handbook on Procedures and Criteria for Determining Refugee Status under the 1951 Convention and the 1967 Protocol relating to the Status of Refugees (HCR/IP/4/Eng/REV.1 Reedited, Geneva, January 1992, UNHCR 1979).

Webber, F. (1993) 'European conventions on immigration and asylum' in T. Bunyan (ed.) *Statewatching the new Europe: a handbook on the European State* (Statewatch), p. 142.

A British View of the European Budget

Roger Liddle

When I became European policy adviser to Tony Blair in 1997, I was left in no doubt by British officials and experts on the European Union's budget that two central and related principles were at the heart of British governmental attitudes towards this issue. The first and probably more important was that the existing arrangements for the British rebate/abatement on this country's contribution to the Union's budget could not in any circumstances be a matter for negotiation. Without the abatement, the United Kingdom would find itself making an unreasonably large net contribution to the Union's finances, a contribution much greater than that of comparable countries such as France or Italy. Quite apart from the intrinsic inequity of such an outcome, it would be extremely damaging to the domestic and even international standing of the incoming Labour government if it permitted the restructuring of an arrangement so beneficial to the UK, which had so painfully been negotiated by one of Mr. Blair's Conservative predecessors, namely Mrs. Thatcher.

The second fundamental principle of British European budgetary thinking in the late 1990s was that the overall level of European expenditure should be kept as low as possible, both to reduce the British net contribution to the Union's budget and because the British Treasury, doubting the real usefulness of the European programmes that the UK might access, was often reluctant to make available the 'co-financing' needed from national resources to attract such European spending to this country. In individual cases, the Treasury could show itself more flexible than this strict philosophy allowed, for instance to secure European funding for the disadvantaged (and sometimes not so disadvantaged) British regions. In general, however, the UK saw itself as being firmly in the camp of those urging ever greater discipline and restraint in the evolution of the EU's budget, normally allying itself with like-minded partners such as the Dutch, the Swedes and the Germans.

I thought at the time, and I still think, that these two budgetary principles, while defensible taken separately, constituted together a purely defensive view of the European budget and were indeed a recipe for the perpetuation of a distinctly sub-optimal European budgetary system, of which the necessity for the British rebate was one obvious manifestation. This defensive British thinking was well exemplified by the demonic status awarded in much official British rhetoric to the Common Agricultural Policy (CAP), seen as the source of all the European Union's budgetary problems and particularly of the structural net imbalance in the British unadjusted contribution to the European budget. The substantial benefits accruing to French farmers from the policy have always been widely publicized by press and politicians alike in the UK. Although it was never official British government policy to advocate the abolition of the CAP, many of our partners, including our French partners, believed that it was, and I could well understand why they might have come to that conclusion.

My own view as adviser to the Prime Minister was that the EU certainly needed a CAP, not least for the maintenance of the internal market, in which traded agricultural products play so large a role. It was intellectually lazy and politically naïve of the British government to allow itself for too long to be depicted as the unbridled enemy of the CAP, an enemy motivated moreover in the eyes of its neighbours largely by penny-pinching considerations of its own selfish budgetary interests. I shared in the 1990s the frustration and concerns of many commentators, not just in the UK, at the anomalies and inadequacies of the CAP as it had traditionally functioned. But I argued within the corridors of Whitehall that if the British government was really interested in reforming the CAP, it needed to adopt an altogether more generous and sophisticated approach to the issue. A reformed CAP was certainly a reasonable and achievable goal of British policy, and that would in its turn probably help reduce the net British contribution to the EU, but the diplomatic and political framework within which such a case was made to our partners would be crucial to the success or otherwise of the enterprise.

Over the years, I think that the case I was arguing made an increasing impact in British governmental circles. In particular, I think that Mr. Blair was coming to accept that the willingness to discuss the terms of the British rebate/abatement would be seen by many of our partners as a gesture of good faith on our part, and would thus strengthen rather than weaken our negotiating hand. The concept of a ‘grand bargain’ between himself and Mr. Chirac, whereby a reduction of the payments made to French farmers from the CAP was ‘traded’ against the British rebate/abatement in the context of a radical restructuring of the EU’s budget, was one in which I know he was interested at the time of the British Presidency of 2005. By that time, however, two further complicating factors had entered the equation, the damage caused to Anglo-French relations by the Iraq war and the impact on the European budget caused by the Union’s enlargement. The first of these made considerably more difficult the prospect of a ground-breaking agreement between Mr. Blair and Mr. Chirac. The second radically, and to some extent unpredictably, changed the whole context of European budgetary negotiations.

As is well known, the British government has always been an enthusiastic supporter of the enlargement of the Union. Its approach, however, to the budgetary consequences of this enlargement has not always gained the sympathy of either the new or existing members of the Union. New members have viewed with suspicion the British argument that direct payments to them from the Union's budget should be phased in over time, as their national administrations become better able to make effective use of these new resources. Existing members have firmly rejected the British suggestion that in future transfers between richer and poorer members of the Union, notably the Central and Eastern European countries, should primarily take place on a netted-out cash basis. The German government has been especially vocal in its insistence that there must continue to be specific European projects, demonstrably funded by the Union, carried out in Germany, above all in the former East Germany. Probably rightly, the German government believes that German electors will be more willing to bear the overall burden of financial transfers to Eastern and Central Europe if it can be shown that some of the benefits of these programmes accrue to their own country as well.

All these issues came to a head in the budgetary negotiations of 2005. The objective consequence of enlargement was, in the short term, to make more difficult any radical reform of the European budget, as both new and longer-established members of the Union sought to defend their legitimate interests and their anticipated advantages. As part of a complicated compromise, it was agreed by the European Council that a wide-ranging review of the European Union's budget would be set up in 2008 to make recommendations for the next set of long-term budgetary negotiations in 2012. The European Council clearly hoped that by that stage greater stability and consensus could be achieved in national attitudes to the future workings of the Union's budget. Significantly from the British point of view, the Council agreed in 2005 on a different method of calculating the British rebate/abatement, whereby the arrangement would no longer apply to 'those elements of Community expenditure which related to new member states.' This was in response to an effective campaign mounted by the new member states in protest at what they saw as their contribution to the British rebate/abatement, a campaign which embarrassed the British government and gained predictable sympathy from those of Britain's partners who themselves are far from enthusiastic contributors to the British rebate/abatement.

The budgetary review set up by the European Council of 2005 will have its work cut out. Theoretical willingness to consider radical reform, espoused in rhetoric by many national governments, will not necessarily be translated into reality. The limited success of British negotiating tactics in the period leading up to the agreement in 2005 is a warning to all governments of the need to consider a wide range of perceived national interests in the development of negotiating tactics likely to be uccessful and persuasive. I see three main challenges facing the review.

The first is the continuing reform of the CAP. My own preference would be for the substantial reform of the cereal sector, concentrating on what I see as the excessive payments to large cereal farmers. This is an important part of the CAP but sufficiently specific and limited an area of reform to be potentially achievable. The second urgent issue is that there remains inadequate funding for a number of expenditures that are undoubtedly best implemented at the European level. I would mention in this context specifically research and development, the European Neighbourhood Policy, the protection of the Union's common external borders and, above all, climate change. The recognition of these European priorities needs to be reinforced with a new emphasis placed upon them in the formation of future EU budgets. Finally, I would like to see a greater linkage between the Union's budget and current EU economic and social reform programmes. The current financial crisis has made the argument for this linkage more compelling than ever before. Over the coming years the Union will undoubtedly need to prop up certain of its members to overcome the most acute problems in their public finances. It would make eminent good sense for this support not simply to confine itself to the present difficulties of these national governments, but to be structured in such a way as to encourage those governments to plan and reform for the long term. Reformed labour markets and enlightened national social policies are the keys to the European Union's future. The European Union's budget can and should be structured in such a way as to facilitate the realization of these twin goals.

Another View of the European Budget: Submission by Federal Trust to European Commission for Budget Review, April 2008

Brendan Donnelly

Many commentators and some national governments believe that the review of the European budget currently taking place will usher in an era of radical change for the Union's financial affairs. There is indeed a widespread sense among governments and voters that the European Union's budget is today largely a product of its past history, lacking contemporary legitimacy and only approximately related to the Union's present needs and challenges. Few would deny the appropriateness of a fundamental reconsideration of the intellectual and political basis on which the European budget currently stands. This submission is a contribution to such a reconsideration. It is divided into three parts: a summary review of the principal political premises which frame the budgetary debate; a brief analysis of current political and academic proposals for budgetary reform; and a package of reforms which, taken together, seek to address many of the voiced concerns about the Union's current budget.

Five General Principles Underlying the Debate

1. Most EU governments, particularly those from the bigger and more prosperous member states, are now much more inclined than they were twenty or even ten years ago to consider in their approach to the European budget the statistical relationship between their country's contribution to and its direct financial benefit from the EU budget. Any proposal which is likely over time to worsen this relationship for any individual country will be met with the greatest scepticism from the country in question. This attitude is rooted in both economic and political considerations. Economic growth in many long-standing members of the Union has slowed considerably since the 1980s. Higher net national payments to the EU budget mean less money to devote to pressing domestic challenges such as healthcare and education. It is on their success or failure in dealing with these questions that the electoral future of national politicians largely depends. Nor are national politicians any longer willing (or probably able) to advocate to their national electorates higher net contributions to the EU simply in the interests of European solidarity. Other national governments and publics have in recent years followed the British example from the 1980s of seeking rebates on their net contributions to the European budget. No reform of the European budget will be politically conceivable for the foreseeable future in

which the calculation of likely net contributions of the individual member states is ignored.

2. It does not follow, however, from the argument of the preceding paragraph that all or even most member states of the Union seek a 'juste retour' from the European budget, if by that phrase is meant a precise equality between every country's payments into and receipts from the European budget. The great majority of member states accept the proposition that the poorest member states should be net beneficiaries of the EU budget. The consequence of this is that the bigger and richer countries in general accept that they should be *to some extent* net contributors to the EU budget, as is the UK after its rebate. The extent of this contribution from wealthier states is and will remain a matter of controversy. Wealthier states will naturally wish to place limits on their per capita net contribution, and the domestic political advocacy of these contributions will be rendered much easier if it can be shown that it is primarily the poorer members of the Union who benefit from the net contributions of the richer member states.

3. Most member states, particularly those which are net contributors, are incomparably more reluctant than they were twenty years ago to see increases in the relative size of the European budget. This is partly due to domestic economic pressures, but partly also due to general doubts about the efficiency and effectiveness of European spending. Those countries that are reconciled to being net contributors are now much more eager than

ever before to be reassured that the budget to which they are net contributors is well spent, both in its day-to-day management and in terms of the political and economic rationale underlying its activities.

4. Although previous budgetary settlements were undoubtedly a reflection of the political and economic circumstances of their own time, they reflect a delicate balance of priorities, constraints and imperatives under which the individual member states act. Though the political figures may have changed in the intervening period, the spirit of the previous negotiated arrangements is the starting-point for the mindset of current political leaders. It is not possible to proceed without some degree of continuity flowing from the previous budget settlements. In particular, national governments will be reluctant to accept that social or economic sectors which in their countries have benefited from the workings of the Union's budget until now should be deprived of those benefits in anything other than the long term.

5. The governments of many, probably most, member states of the EU believe that their national electorates accept or can be persuaded to accept at least existing, or even marginally higher levels of European spending if a plausible case can be made that the policy area covered by this spending will be more effectively, and ideally more cheaply, pursued at the European level rather than at the national level. There are policy areas, such as foreign and defence policy, environmental policy, industrial research, transport and cross-border

infrastructure, where the European component of future effective policy-making is widely accepted by national electorates. A budget which better reflected this acceptance than the current structures would be politically much more congenial and accessible to voters throughout the EU than the present arrangements.

The Current Budget Debate

There is tension, even contradiction, between certain of the preceding principles. Numerous proposals to reform the EU budget have been presented by a variety of academics, committees and member governments. This section groups those suggestions loosely into five groups of proposals, from the analysis of which the report later draws specific elements into a package of recommendations.

1. Proposals to increase significantly the overall size of the budget

Increasing the overall size of the budget could undoubtedly facilitate reform, creating scope to re-orientate expenditure between current areas of expenditure or towards entirely new policy initiatives. The EU budget spends a relatively small proportion of GDP given the range of national policies that have a potentially European dimension. An intellectually respectable case can certainly be made for the proposition that the current and likely future range of European policies can only be rationally pursued on the basis of a much larger central budget for the Union.

As a matter of political reality, however, proposals to increase the size of the budget are unlikely to receive support even from a majority of member states (much less from all of them), especially given the current composition of expenditure. National governments face tight budget constraints at national level and must contain deficits over time within the limits of the Stability and Growth Pact. The distinct tendency of the Union's budget in the past decade has been for the member states to contain its size well below its theoretical limit of 1.27% of EU GDP. There are no conceivable circumstances in which a political consensus could be found in the foreseeable future for any significant upward revision of the EU's existing budgetary resources.

2. Re-nationalisation of elements of budget expenditure

A complete re-nationalisation of certain policies, in particular agricultural support, has been proposed by some to address the unequal burden of the European budget for net contributors. Previous agricultural reforms have shifted CAP spending from production support to direct income payments, creating a more transparent system, for which financial support could equally well come from national exchequers as from the EU. Re-nationalisation would free a large proportion of the EU's budgetary expenditure to dedicate to new policy areas, but with the added advantage that it would potentially render less haphazard the current net contributions among wealthier member states.

Whatever its virtues, this proposal is unlikely to feature as part of the next budget package. Full-scale re-nationalisation of agricultural support would risk undermining the internal market in agricultural products, with different structures of governmental aid to farmers, differing timetables for this aid, and differing inflation rates, reinforced in some cases by currency movements. Re-nationalising farm payments would inevitably encounter great resistance from current beneficiaries of agricultural expenditure, whether from industrial groups, member states or individual farmers, who might fear a reduction in overall levels of support. Moreover, the recent entrants to the EU are not yet receiving the highest level of agricultural payments (as there is an ongoing transitional arrangement) and could be expected strongly to oppose full scale re-nationalisation.

3. Co-financing of budget expenditure

An extension of co-financing between the EU budget and national exchequers has been proposed for certain elements within the budget, in particular as part of a major restructuring of agricultural expenditure. This could be a useful reform for three reasons. Firstly, it would ensure a more equitable distribution of expenditure within the Union, because certain wealthy member states currently benefit disproportionately from direct payments to farmers. Secondly, it could be part of an overall new budgetary settlement whereby all or most wealthy member states end up as small net contributors, thereby giving scope to abolish the complex and opaque rebates system. Thirdly, it would make available significant resources to devote either to common policy goals or to increase the proportion of the EU budget spent in the poorer member states.

Since co-financing would not of itself change the level of overall expenditure on agricultural support nor endanger the continuation of the European dimension to agriculture, this reform would be less likely to be disputed by the agricultural sector. In addition to this, commodities prices, in particular global food prices, have recently been strong, and are expected to remain so for some years at least, a circumstance which presents a window of opportunity for fundamental reform of the EU's agricultural payments system.

4. Reform of rebates system

Rebates granted to the main net-contributor member states have been over the past twenty years an important concession to those member states that believed that the implicit budget bargain was unfairly structured to their disadvantage. This system has resulted in a complex payment structure that is little understood except by those with a specific interest in the field. A number of proposals have been made to abolish the system, and pressure in this direction has increased with the Union's expansion to 27 member states.

However, the small number of member states most directly affected is increasingly unwilling to bear the brunt of the cost of the European budget. Domestic political forces monitor closely the balance of net contributions, in such a way that it is politically unsustainable for a small number of member states to fund a large proportion of the EU budget. In isolation, the rebates system is unlikely to be discontinued, specifically because the net contributors believe the current budget to be unfairly structured. There might however be scope to link the issue of rebates with far-reaching expenditure reforms that result in most or all wealthy member states ending up as modest net contributors.

5. Re-orientation or a re-balance of expenditure across current policy areas or to entirely new areas

The current structure of budget expenditure does little to address the contemporary concerns of Europeans, a defect which adds to the sense that the EU is a remote project, doing little for the ordinary citizen. A fundamental overhaul of expenditure to address some of those concerns could have both symbolic and tangible effects on the relationship between the EU and its citizens.

The most substantive proposal for reforming expenditure has been made by the group of experts chaired by Andre Sapir in 2003. The Sapir Report (2003) has proposed re-orientating the EU budget towards meeting the 2010 Lisbon objective to create a dynamic knowledge-based European economy. The report argues that the budget should be sub-divided into three discrete funds, focused on: growth and research; income convergence across the EU; and re-training for those workers adversely affected by economic change. The Sapir Report also recognises that should the overall size of the budget remain unchanged, agricultural spending would need to be radically reduced or perhaps wholly re-nationalised. As already argued, the last change (wholesale renationalisation) would be politically problematic, but the underlying philosophy of the Sapir report, namely that the goals of the European budget should be demonstrably 'European' goals, is a politically highly attractive one. The proposition that the European

Union's citizens in general would benefit from Europe-wide research projects, from greater income convergence and from retraining for those made unemployed by the economic pressures of enlargement and globalisation is one that might well find a receptive audience among politicians and electors throughout the Union.

Recommendations and Analysis

Recommendation 1: The starting-point for a contemporary European budget should be the underlying philosophy (if not necessarily all the detailed suggestions) of the Sapir report, namely that the European budget should revolve around European solutions for European problems. In particular, a review should be conducted of the European Union's existing budgetary structure with a view to establishing those areas of present or future expenditure which are of 'general European interest' and those which are only of 'sectional European interest'. Those former policies would be those which promise to promote benefits tending to increase the welfare of the citizens of the European Union as a whole. Policies of 'sectional European interest' would be those which benefit only some parts of the European economy, whether geographically or otherwise defined.

Examples of polices of 'general interest' might be initiatives on the environment, elements of CFSP, foreign and pre-accession aid, research and development projects with spill-over benefits, the development of the common market, jobs and growth, and the management of migration. The CAP and cohesion policy would clearly fall within the 'sectional' character of expenditure. It should be the goal of the EU budget in the long term to move towards a budgetary system dominated by 'general' rather than 'sectional' European policies. 'Sectional' policies may have their legitimate place within policies of 'general' interest, but they must demonstrably contribute to the overall realisation of these policies.

Recommendation 2A: Payments for preservation and management of natural resources (agricultural payments) should be co-financed, as cohesion policy is currently. Both policies involve a direct benefit to a member state, region or collective group within one member state, which is not shared equally across the Union as a whole.

Recommendation 2B: In tandem with the extension of co-financing to agricultural payments, the complex system of rebates should either be abolished or substantially reduced to the absolute minimum necessary to avoid glaring anomalies.

The implications of recommendations 2A and 2B need to be examined together, since they constitute the fundamental financial aspects of proposed reforms from the perspective of key national governments. Meeting the financial concerns of these governments is an indispensable precondition for any durable reform of the present EU budget. The major implication of these recommendations would be to free a large proportion of EU budget expenditure (in the region of 18-20%), at least some of which would be available to spend on new, politically attractive and economically rational areas of European initiative. It should be stressed that poorer member states with large agricultural sectors would not necessarily lose by this proposed change since they could expect to receive a substantial proportion of the restructured budget expenditure. It should also be stressed that, at least initially, not all the available new resources would need to be incorporated into the European budget. This incorporation would depend on the development by the Union of worthwhile policies of 'general' European interest on which the resources could be deployed.

A second implication of these twin recommendations would be to establish a greater balance in net contributions to the EU budget among all of the wealthy member states. This would reduce the extent to which certain wealthy member states with large agricultural sectors disproportionately benefit from current budget expenditure. Those member states would tend under the new system to gravitate towards the desirable position of becoming modest net contributors. If all or most wealthy member states were to end up as modest net contributors, there would much less justification for a system of rebates within the budgetary arrangements. The abolition of the rebate system, or at the very least its radical curtailment, would of itself be a very welcome consequence of the proposed extension of co-financing to agricultural payments.

The precise impact of extending co-financing to agricultural expenditure on national budgets merits, however, in this context, further discussion. If national exchequers maintained under a co-financing system the same overall level of financial support for their agricultural sectors as they have enjoyed until now, this proposed reform would increase the level of public expenditure in those wealthy member states with larger agricultural sectors, which would in its turn significantly impact on their national budgets. The extent to which these national budgets would suffer a net financial loss (under this recommendation) would of course be lessened by the removal of the system of rebates, since it is those states that anyway largely fund the current rebate system. Furthermore, other benefits would flow from increased European expenditure in areas of new priority which might in future lower domestic expenditure on those policies in the countries affected. The real financial value of EU agricultural payments has in any case been falling over time and is likely to continue to do so. The burden of agricultural co-financing can reasonably be expected to be a diminishing one.

Despite these mitigating factors, on balance the wealthy member states with large agricultural sectors would face increased national budget expenditure as a result of recommendations 2A and 2B. In order to facilitate the adjustment to extended co-financing on European agricultural expenditure, this proposed reform might well need to be phased in over a number of years, thus allowing national budgets to adjust over time. This gradual process of adjustment necessary for the implementation of significant changes to the Union's budget is one powerful reason for Recommendation 3 below, which seeks to change the current system of the Union's medium-term financial planning, which is unnecessarily inflexible.

Recommendation 3: The current system of the 'Medium Term Financial Perspective' (MTFP) should be reformed to facilitate necessary changes in the Union's budgetary arrangements, not least consistent increases in the proportion of the EU budget spent on polices of 'general European interest'. No single MTFP should last longer than three years.

Under the present budgetary system of the Union, every seven years a new MTFP is adopted; a process which substantially determines the Union's financial architecture throughout the next seven years. This is an incomparably longer time horizon than that adopted by any national government, and militates significantly against substantial budgetary reform or even refinement. After seven years, disequilibria in the Union's budget tend to become self-sustaining rather than self-correcting. The system is also vulnerable to the hazards of highly personalised negotiations in the European Council, when temporary alliances or congruence of interest can set the terms of the European budget for many years to come beyond any real prospect of alteration. A shorter period for future MTFPs would ensure greater flexibility, and enable those participating in the financial negotiations to review progress towards desirable budgetary goals more regularly.

Above all, more regular reviews of the MTFPs would allow the continuing re-allocation of the Union's resources towards 'general interest' areas of highest political priority. These areas should reflect contemporary concerns of European citizens and member governments, in policy areas with a publicly demonstrable European dimension. This essay argues that policies to benefit the environment, to promote jobs and growth across the single market and to reinforce the Union's external role would be the most appropriate and politically relevant focal points for the future budget of the Union. A newly focused budget would send an important symbolic message that European leaders are listening to the concerns of ordinary citizens, and are responding by setting aside new resources to fund policies that help to secure a safer, more prosperous and environmentally sustainable future.

Recommendation 4: It should be a specific goal of the new budgetary system that expenditures and national contributions should over time reflect a modestly redistributive philosophy for the Union's budget. When new financial perspectives are drawn up, the expected pattern of national contributions and expenditure should reflect this philosophy for the future and look to correct unexpected or perverse outcomes in the previous period.

The fourth recommendation is designed to ensure a continuing focus on the progressive and redistributive dimension of the EU budget when agreeing the multi-annual financial perspectives. If implemented, the reform package suggested in this paper would in any case devote more expenditure to 'general interest' policies, while spreading the net costs of the EU budget more widely. This development should of itself lessen the political focus on the 'juste retour' accruing to individual member states. However, the issue of respective national contributions is likely to retain high political significance, so that ensuring the budget's progressive dimension should not be left to chance. The workings of both 'general' and 'sectional' EU expenditure in the budget should be designed and reviewed in such a way as to reflect the modestly financially-progressive principle, whereby poorer countries (in terms of relative levels of per capita income) are normally net beneficiaries, and the richer countries are normally net contributors, particularly in the longer term.

Conclusion

The above recommendations, taken as a package, would substantially alter the composition of the EU budget, in a manner consonant with the outlined principles drawn from the current political and economic debate. A clearer purpose for the budget, primarily to fund 'general interest' policies that benefit the majority of EU citizens, would emerge. This package would retain, and probably in the short term reduce, the current size of the budget. The net cost of the package would be spread between the wealthy member states with larger agricultural sectors, and those in receipt of rebates. The expenditure side would also be restructured to include new policy goals, but with careful consideration of the impact of these new policies on poorer member states. This focus on new, politically attractive policy goals is of crucial importance to building a coalition across member states and European institutions that favours substantial reform, ideally along the lines of proposals set out in this essay. Agreement, however, on theoretically desirable policy goals for the future European budget will not of itself suffice to promote reform. A politically and institutionally plausible 'roadmap' is necessary to sketch out the implementing changes necessary for such reform to become politically plausible in the European Council. Any discussion of abstractly desirable goals for the Union's budget, however sophisticated, needs to be firmly grounded in an equally sophisticated analysis of the political and economic calculations which will lead 27 national leaders eventually to endorse reform. This submission has been an attempt to help the Union's national leaders to make these calculations in a way they would find palatable.

New Social Dimensions of Europe[1]

Frédéric Lerais

Introduction

The social situation has changed in Europe, and citizens have great expectations regarding the European Union. This is the reason why a vast consultation for a 'social reality check' was launched by the European Commission in February 2007. This exercise was announced in the European Commission 'Citizen's agenda' on 10 May 2006.[2] The process was inaugurated with three seminars with a local focus – Dublin, Paris, Budapest – a specific Eurobarometer on 'Social reality'[3] and a discussion paper on 'Europe's social reality' by Roger Liddle and Frédéric Lerais. The Commission consultation ran until mid-February 2008 and in July 2008, as a result of the vast consultation, a renewed social agenda was adopted.

In this essay, I will describe what the main social challenges in Europe are and the responses the EU Commission propose. In the first section, I will give some elements of background of the renewed social agenda. In the second section, I will describe the main social trends as identified in the social reality report. The third section introduces the analysis put forward by the European Commission, that feeds into the renewed social agenda, released in July 2008.

Where Does the Social Reality Exercise Stem From?

Already some social policies are in place in the EU. The main responsibility in this area is not in the hands of the EU but in those of the Member States. But it is clear that action at European level is key to a coordinated development in the EU. At the beginning of this Commission, there was an intensive debate about the European social model, which gave rise to a fruitful discussion at the Hampton Court informal summit in October 2005.

Following this discussion and the Dutch and French referenda, the Commission announced in the 'Citizen's agenda' of 10 May 2006 three reports to improve European policies: (i) The Single Market Review; (ii) The Budget Review and (iii) A consultation on the social reality stock-taking. A vast consultation was then launched on social reality with a view to taking 'comprehensive stock of the reality and to launch a new social agenda on access and opportunities'.[4]

During this exercise, the Commission was in a 'listening mode'. The objective was to understand what is important in today's Europe social reality before proposing political options. The object of this process is to check the level of agreement on the social challenges Europe has to face amongst Europeans.

Subjective Well-being

To start with, we look in our findings at subjective indicators related to well-being. Well-being of citizens cannot be reduced to subjective indicators. Nonetheless, it is a convenient way of summarising complex information. If we look at subjective indicators, we get a paradoxical picture of Europe. According to Eurobarometer survey[5], overall, EU citizens are happy with their personal life: 87% of Europeans are satisfied with their everyday life (Table 1). This is a striking result. There are some disparities between Member States. The Netherlands and Denmark appear to be the happiest, followed by most of the Western European states and then the Eastern European states, in which happiness was still at an overall 70%. The heterogeneity in Europe reflects, but only partially, GDP per head.

By contrast, EU citizens are quite pessimistic about the perception of the future. The contrast is really striking compared to the previous indicator since only 17% of European citizens believe that their children will have an easier life than the one they live (Table 2). This raises serious question about intergenerational equity and the perceptions of social progress. Here again, there is heterogeneity in perceptions among Member States. We observe a reverse picture of the previous one on current happiness: The newest recruits to the EU are

Table 1: Happiness Indicators

Question: Taking all things together would you say you are...?

Answer: Happy

Country Results	
Denmark	97%
The Netherlands	95%
Belgium	94%
Ireland	94%
Sweden	94%
Luxembourg	93%
Finland	93%
United Kingdom	92%
Spain	90%
France	90%
Malta	90%
Slovenia	89%
European Union (25)	87%
Cyprus	87%
Czech Republic	87%
Portugal	86%
Poland	86%
Italy	84%
Germany	82%
Austraia	81%
Greece	80%
Slovakia	77%
Estonia	75%
Lithuania	74%
Latvia	72%
Hungary	68%

Other Countries	
Romania	60%
Bulgaria	39%

Table 2: Anticipated Life for Future Generations

Question: Generally speaking, do you think that the life of those who are children today will be easier, more difficult or neither easier nor more difficult than the life of those from your own generation?

Answer: Easier

Country Results	
Portugal	57%
Lithuania	51%
Finland	46%
Ireland	44%
Latvia	44%
Poland	31%
Slovakia	29%
Cyprus	28%
Estonia	28%
Spain	27%
Hungary	24%
Denmark	22%
European Union (25)	17%
Austria	16%
United Kingdom	16%
Italy	15%
Czech Republic	15%
Luxumbourg	14%
The Netherlands	14%
Slovenia	14%
Belgium	13%
Greece	13%
Malta	10%
France	8%
Sweden	8%
Germany	3%

Other Countries	
Romania	36%
Bulgaria	22%

more optimistic about the future. In the Baltic States, in Lithuania 51% of the respondents believe that the future will be easier for their children, in Latvia 44%, and in Estonia 28%.

All in all, this gap between the perception of the future and the present satisfaction is the starting point of our analysis. This gap comes from various social changes in Europe, changes that often cause concerns.

Social Trends Shaping Europe

What are the trends which are shaping Europe's social reality? In the report we have identified five major factors which may influence perceptions of well-being.

Globalisation

The first trend shaping Europe that often comes to mind is globalisation. Globalisation has, indeed, contributed to altering our societies. It has an impact on the demand for skills (with fewer unskilled jobs being available); on migration and even on natural resources. There are also impacts on specific areas when there is outsourcing or 'relocation'. This is a cause of worries.

All in all, the EU gains from trade and globalisation but this is not felt locally where losses can be registered as low skilled jobs are subject to new international competition, where outsourcing creates local job losses, migratory flows increase and where there is more pressure on energy and natural resources.

However, even though globalisation has a major impact, it is not the only factor to take into account when we analyse social changes in Europe. There are at least four major other trends, mainly internally driven.

Service and Knowledge Economy

Firstly, the industrial society has shifted towards a service and knowledge society with fast changes in occupational structure. Nowadays, two third of jobs are in services. Some studies estimate that almost 40% of jobs are in the knowledge sector. In a dynamic perspective, it is still more impressive. In the European economies between 2000 and 2004, 1.7 million industrial jobs and 1.1 million jobs in agriculture have disappeared. By contrast, in the service sector there has been a gain of nearly 8 million jobs.

To face this challenge, there is a growing need of specific skills. Countries in Europe are not always in a good position to meet these challenges: 1 in 6 young people leave school early. And educational outcomes are sometimes very poor, despite the overall increase in educational attainment as recorded in OECD surveys. Moreover, in spite of the decrease of unemployment in the last 10 years, youth unemployment remains very high, with a rate twice as high as the average population.

The Role of Welfare States

Secondly, the impressive rise in life expectancy could be considered as one of the best outcomes of the welfare states: Better health services and pensions plus the abolition of absolute poverty. It is a dramatic European achievement. Life expectancy has increased for men from 43.5 years around 1900 to 75.5 in 2000 and it is forecast to reach 82 in 2050. Of course the gain is not evenly distributed among Member States or among groups of population within the Member States.

In the same time, welfare states, as pension systems, lead to new dependencies. For instance a large number of people aged between 55 and 60 have dropped out of the labour market. Furthermore, relative poverty persists among old people and children. Nearly 12 million of 72 million pensioners are at risk of poverty. Child poverty rate is around 17% in Europe (18 million of children out 94m.). This phenomenon is even increasing in some Member states.

Demographic Trends

Thirdly, there has been a dramatic decrease in the fertility rate from an average of 2.69 in the sixties to 1.5 now, which is below the reproduction rate. The biggest recent falls in fertility have been observed in the new Member States and southern Europe. One can notice a strong correlation between fertility rates, the availability of childcare, easier maternity and paternity leave and the proportion of women in the labour market. Women with stable jobs are more likely to have children.

Of course, those demographic trends have a dramatic impact on social expenditures. Age-related expenditures are expected to soar by 2.5% of GDP by 2030 and 4.3% by 2050. But besides, there are also societal challenges which are not easy to tackle. Let me mention a few of them: (i) 28% over 70s currently live alone, 40% of over 80s; (ii) Up to two thirds of Europeans over 75 are dependent on informal care; (iii) Extended families' care for elderly is weakening; it will weaken even more if people stay at work longer.

Migration can be source of labour supply to partially offset the consequences of demographic trends. But migrants pose also serious challenges. They are often discriminated against in the labour markets. They have often poor educational attainments and their integration is often problematic. The situation is complex in terms of public perceptions. In particular, neither a strong economy nor a particular social model can guarantee success.

Changes in Values: New Wants, New Needs

Finally, in most member states, material needs are increasingly satisfied. But new needs and new wants are emerging. Consumers have new demands in terms of leisure, fitness, tourism, health… Meanwhile, we witness an increase of the consumer's role. There is in many Member States a rise in households' debt. The demand for more personalized and consumer accountable public as well as private services is growing as well as the awareness of risk.

At the same time, we have seen tremendous changes in value along three axes: (i) Increasing secularization and decline of religious belief; (ii) Decline in civic engagement and trust in politics (Social capital); (iii) Demand for greater personal freedom. All this may have an impact on the governance of policies.

In a nutshell Europe becomes more diverse, people face different social risks, the world moves at a higher speed, is more knowledge-driven and the population is ageing rapidly.

What Kind of Responses?

One of the consequences of the combination of characteristics is that future well-being does not only depend on economic activities. Future policies should therefore aim at achieving: the highest possible education for all; a rapid entry into the labour market; the highest labour participation possible; well integrated migrants that add value to European societies; healthy citizens; and citizens fully participating in civil society. These requirements are not needed for social reasons only but for economic reasons too. Healthier, better educated and participating citizens create higher growth.

A big part of the answer relies on the Lisbon Strategy for Growth and Jobs as well as on social inclusion. A modernization of the approach regarding the labour market is in prospect through the flexicurity approach. The renewed social agenda proposes a modernization in many fields of social policies with a focus on social investment.

Lisbon Strategy for Growth and Jobs

According to demographic projections, there is still a 10-year window of opportunity for a rise in employment when taking the current demographic trends into account. Employment growth is possible up to 2017 in Europe since raising employment rates can compensate for the declining working-age population. Thereafter growth has to be achieved through an increase in productivity. This explains why the Lisbon objectives put a priority on the level of employment and on productivity. The employment strategy also stresses active ageing. The Open Method of Coordination on social protection and social inclusion establishes common objectives and reporting on adequate and sustainable pensions and more recently on health and long-term care as part of the Lisbon Strategy.

Flexicurity

This concept of flexicurity is now central in the EU employment and social modernisation. It is an integrated strategy to enhance at the same time flexibility and security in the labour market build on four components: (i) Flexible and secure contractual arrangements from the perspective of the employers and the employees. This clearly means that flexibility is about more than 'hire and fire': internal flexibility is as important as external flexibility; (ii) Active labour market policies that promote 'Transition Security'; (iii) Reliable and responsible lifelong learning systems that enhance employability and raise productivity ; (iv) Modern social security systems that combine adequate income support with the need to promote labour market mobility.

The concept has been sometimes misperceived. It is key to recall that flexicurity is not a bargaining position; the final aim of the concept is to increase 'security' overall. Studies clearly show that the feeling of security relies more on helping and encouraging unemployed people and on the number of job opportunities than on the level of employment benefits or the strictness of labour protection.[6] It calls for a cross-cutting strategy. This is a key point to facilitate change.

The Renewed Social Agenda

At the beginning of July 2008 the European Commission adopted a communication concluding the 'social reality' exercise.[7] This communication puts forward a number of political options as responses to the new social challenges previously described.

At the core of these political options there are three words: Opportunity (i.e. means to promote life chances at an early stage), Access (i.e. giving access to services, to education, labour markets, health services), and Solidarity (i.e. promoting second chances and cohesion). In other words, it puts the stress on youth life chances and social investment as a mean to tackle many of the issues already mentioned. The core objective is to promote life chances by giving a 'strong start'; in giving access to services, to education, labour markets, health services and in offering a second chance to those who need it.

The communication highlighted also the idea of 'social investment' in a number of areas. Young people are at the centre of the approach. The idea behind this approach is that social policies should not put so much stress on repairing damage but rather on prevention or on building human and social capital. A policy should be assessed on the long-lasting effects on individuals and on society. Many studies show for instance that inequity, poverty etc. are better fought when addressed early on. Typically, this approach is backed by work of the Nobel

Prize laureate James Heckman. Equipping young people brings long-term social returns.

What is new in this communication is to address the situation of young people, their mobility and improving their chances of success as a core question. It sets the need to view social policy in terms of social investment. Put simply, this means not just solving problems, but rather anticipating a number of problems. It emphasises the concept of life chances, underlining nevertheless that it is not possible to guarantee better chances or greater opportunities in life, without at the same time taking initiatives to encourage access to certain services, in particular education, so that these life chances can be realised and to ensure greater solidarity.

This communication sets out seven areas for social investment. It establishes that more resources must be focussed on education for young children, equality between the sexes, health and professional transitions.

The Role of the EU

Until now we have not raised the issue of competence of the EU or Member States. Indeed we are in an area of shared competences and we recognize that for many of the areas mentioned (areas linked to education, social protection and other areas) the margin for manoeuvre and levers of social policy are particular to each country. The EU has only a complementary competence in these areas, yet there are reasons to believe that the EU offers a real added value, *inter alia* by providing a more dynamic view of difficult issues for Member States.

Even though the Member States hold the main responsibilities, the European Commission has identified five ways to help catalyse these objectives. They are first setting and reaching common objectives; secondly raising awareness and building strong knowledge bases; thirdly, sharing experiences and practices to inspire policy makers; fourthly supporting local, regional, national action (Structural funds, Globalisation funds) and finally setting a legal framework (for e.g. anti-discrimination, free movement)

The most obvious areas for EU intervention are associated with open coordination methods that consist of setting and achieving shared objectives. This has worked in a number of cases, perhaps not always in terms of specific results, but has made it possible to shed new light on a number of themes. What is clearly essential in this process is the sharing of experiences and good practices between countries. Also suggested in the communication is that support on a local level, through structural funds, is very important. The question now is how to connect these structural funds with a new approach to social investment.

Conclusion

In conclusion, what are the lessons we can draw from this stocktaking exercise? Europe becomes more diverse, people face different social risks, the world moves at a higher speed, is more knowledge-driven and the population is ageing rapidly.

The consequence of this combination of characteristics is that future well-being does not only depend on economic activities. Contrary to common presumptions, the changes do not only come from 'outside' or stem from globalisation. Changes lie at the root of growth and prosperity.

For changes to become opportunities people need to adapt and institutions have to facilitate change. For citizens to be able to adapt, they need to overcome their concern that changes form a threat. For institutions to facilitate change, knowledge about what works and what does not is key, and needs to be complemented with political vision and leadership.

The EU approach derived from the social reality check makes a strong case for more social investment with a focus on youth. Invest in pre-school education. Reduce early school leaving. Get more people into higher education. Promote rapid entry into the labour market. Make sure everybody is equipped for life-long learning.

All this calls for going beyond the traditional trade-off between economic and social policies, in which social policies are created to 'correct' economic outcomes. Modern social policies are to be an input for future well-being by being preventive, pro-active and remedial only as a last resort, based on shared responsibilities between stakeholders.

Notes

1 This essay draws heavily on Roger Liddle and Frédéric Lerais, 2007: 'A consultation paper from the Bureau of European Policy Advisers. Europe's social reality'. The essay summarises a presentation made in Riga, 6 November 2008.

2 COM (2006) 211 final 'A citizen's agenda delivering result for Europe'. Brussels, 10 May 2006.

3 Special Eurobarmeter (2007). *European Social Reality.*

4 COM (2006) 211 op. cit

5 Special Eurobarmeter (2007). *European Social Reality.*

6 OECD (2007): 'Employment outlook'.

7 COM (2008) 412 final. 'Renewed social agenda: Opportunities, access and solidarity in 21st century Europe'. See also COM (2007) 726 final. 'Opportunities, access and solidarity: towards a new social vision for 21st century Europe'.

The Lisbon Treaty and British Reactions to It

Brendan Donnelly

The European Councils of 2007 which adopted the Lisbon Treaty were hopeful that the Treaty could be ratified and brought into operation by the end of 2008. This optimistic timetable was destroyed by the Irish referendum of 13th June, 2008, with its substantial majority against the Treaty. This article reviews the events leading up to and following from the Irish referendum, and attempts to analyze the consequences for the British debate on the European Union arising from the outcome of the Irish referendum.

The Irish Referendum

There were obvious points of similarity between the French and Dutch referendums of 2005 and the Irish referendum of 2008. In all three cases, the advocates of the new European treaties fought a lacklustre and often complacent campaign. Jaundiced electorates in all three countries took the opportunity to rebuke their unpopular political elites on what seemed to many a marginal and technical issue. Moreover, public discussion of the Treaties was, in France, the Netherlands and Ireland, frequently centred on matters unrelated to the texts at issue. On the day after the results of the French, Irish and Dutch referendums were announced, political leaders of these countries had received from their electors no politically coherent critique of the Treaties proposed. This last factor was an important reason why the French and Dutch governments were unable for many months after their national referendums to devise any politically or intellectually coherent response to the rebuff they had suffered. After the Irish referendum of 2008, the Irish government found itself confronted with a similarly diffuse and even contradictory range of popular objections to the Lisbon Treaty.

There were, however, important differences between the circumstances of 2005 and those of 2008. Other referendums, of uncertain outcome, were due to follow the French and Dutch referendums. National governments were unwilling to press ahead with these further referendums until the impasse produced by the French and Dutch referendums had been resolved. The British government in particular was swift to suspend its ratification procedures for the European Constitutional Treaty, a step which of itself probably marked the demise of that Treaty. By contrast, in 2008, no further national referendums on the Lisbon Treaty were scheduled to follow the Irish referendum. Those national governments who had either already completed their national ratification procedures, or were about to do so, were not slow to point out to the Irish government that 110,000 Irish voters, the margin of victory in their referendum, were in effect preventing the implementation of a decision painfully negotiated and ratified by the democratically-elected representatives of hundreds of millions of voters throughout the EU. For the great majority of Ireland's partners in the EU, the onus was firmly upon the Irish government to make proposals for the rectification of an anomalous situation which it itself had played at least some part in causing.

The Irish government was aware of the delicacy and complexity of the situation in which it found itself. It did not say, as it might have done, that Ireland would withdraw from the Lisbon Treaty. It did not say that the Treaty should be abandoned. The Irish government had been a full participant in the negotiations leading up to the Treaty, it believed the Treaty was advantageous for Ireland and it knew how fragile was the compromise it represented. Essentially, the Irish government spent the second half of 2008 asking its partners to give it more time to find a way out of the political quandary in which Ireland and the EU found themselves.

Understandable although it was that the Irish government should wish to avoid any hasty commitments on the subject, it was from the first very difficult to see any other way out of the impasse other than a second Irish referendum on the Lisbon Treaty, superseding the result of the first. For the Lisbon Treaty eventually to come into force, it was and is necessary that all signatories of the Treaty should complete their national processes of ratification. The Irish government was in the autumn of 2008 unable to do so. Three possible responses were logically open to it. It could accept the destruction of the Treaty by the Irish referendum vote, it could negotiate an arrangement whereby Ireland withdrew from the Treaty of Lisbon but allowed its implementation by others, or it could hold a second referendum to reverse the result of the first. The first of these options was politically highly unattractive to the government in Dublin, damaging as it would have been to its relations with all its most important economic and political partners in the EU. The second was technically extremely difficult and politically likely to be only marginally less damaging to Irish interests than the first. By a process of elimination, only the third possibility, that of a second referendum, remained as a realistic option to the Irish government. From the autumn of 2008, that was clearly the solution of its European dilemma towards which the Irish government was cautiously advancing.

The Irish government's caution was understandable. There was and is no guarantee that a second referendum can be won. A second referendum could well expose the government to accusations from its critics of arrogance and bad faith for its attempt to overturn the popular decision expressed in the referendum of June, 2008. A second referendum might well fuel whatever sense currently exists in Ireland of estrangement between the institutions of the EU and the average European citizen, who supposedly finds his concerns about and aspirations for the process of European integration systematically ignored by the purblind elites of Brussels, Strasbourg and national capitals. The Irish government would need to prepare the ground, both in Ireland and with its European partners, before launching itself on the hazardous enterprise of a second referendum.

The Irish government, however, was not without political and rhetorical weapons to deploy in defending its new stance. As a democratically-elected Irish government, it had freely signed the Lisbon Treaty on behalf of its fellow citizens. Irish negotiators had played a leading part in the drafting and negotiation of the final Treaty. The Treaty's text was not in any sense a document imposed on the Irish government by the European Commission or other national governments. Opinion polls after the Irish referendum showed beyond any reasonable doubt that a number of demonstrable misconceptions and misunderstandings about the Lisbon Treaty contributed significantly to the negative outcome of the Irish referendum. The Irish government has argued, and continues to argue, that there is nothing democratically inappropriate in the government's now making a further effort of explanation and persuasion about the Treaty it signed in what it believed and believes were its country's best interests. It is far from obvious what theory of democracy might dictate that in no circumstances should the Irish electorate be given the opportunity to change its mind on a European issue such as the Lisbon Treaty. Indeed, if the Irish electorate is genuinely outraged by the prospect of a second referendum on the Lisbon Treaty, it will have the opportunity of demonstrating this outrage by voting against the Treaty even more decisively than it did in 2008.

As the months have passed since the Irish referendum, Ireland's partners have shown themselves increasingly willing to do what they can to help the Irish government win a second referendum, now likely to take place in the autumn of 2009. Without renegotiating the Treaty of Lisbon, they have been willing to provide reassurances and interpretations of the Treaty helpful to the Irish government on matters such as corporate tax rates, divorce, the WTO and Irish neutrality, all of which were issues raised during the Irish referendum campaign, but to which the Lisbon Treaty either had no relevance or a relevance unrelated to the public debate. More substantially, Ireland's partners have agreed not to apply the reduction in the number of Commissioners envisaged by the Nice and Lisbon Treaties, a reduction which many Irish voters hostile to the Lisbon Treaty apparently feared would work to Ireland's disadvantage. It is widely believed in Brussels and in national capitals that the European Commission is currently too large a body to function effectively. The European Council has clearly concluded that the maintenance of this unwieldy body in its current composition is a price worth paying to encourage the desired result in a second Irish referendum. To any accusations that the Council is attempting by this reversal of previous decisions to 'bribe' the Irish electorate with the guarantee of a well-paid and influential position in Brussels for one of its citizens, the Council's members can justly retort that they have been listening to the concerns of ordinary Irish electors, a practice of which their critics frequently complain that they are incapable.

At the time of writing, it appears likely that the Irish government will be able to win a second referendum on the Lisbon Treaty, to be held in the last quarter of 2009. The assurances given and concessions made by Ireland's partners in recent months seem to have changed Irish perceptions of the Lisbon Treaty. Many observers also believe that the current healthy majority predicted for the 'Yes' camp in the next Irish referendum on the Lisbon Treaty is particularly a consequence of the current widespread economic uncertainty in the Irish Republic, an uncertainty which (on this analysis) may well discourage Irish voters from causing further uncertainty in their country's relations with its influential neighbours and trading partners.

British Attitudes to the Lisbon Treaty

To the surprise of many observers, the British government did not use the negative result of the Irish referendum on the Treaty in June as an excuse for suspending the British ratification procedure. A number of factors will have weighed with Mr. Blair's successor as Prime Minister, Mr. Brown, in deciding to pursue this course. The British ratification procedure was nearly completed by the time of the Irish referendum, needing only the approval of the House of Lords. For Mr. Brown to have stopped the House of Lords from taking the last step to complete the British process of ratification would have been widely seen as a success for his domestic opponents. Mr. Brown had been much criticized for his absence in late 2007 from the general signing ceremony of the Lisbon Treaty. To complete the British ratification of the Lisbon Treaty, despite the Irish rejection of that Treaty, may well have seemed to him an indication of renewed firmness of purpose in his European policy. He may also have calculated that a rapid conclusion of the ratification procedure would create a difficult tactical dilemma for the major British party of opposition to his government, the Conservatives.

In this last calculation, Mr. Brown seems to have been at least partly correct. Pointing to the undeniable similarities between the European Constitutional Treaty and the Lisbon Treaty, the Conservative Party has consistently argued that a referendum should be held on the latter document in the United Kingdom, as part of the new Treaty's process of ratification. After initial hesitation, Mr. Blair had expressed his willingness to hold a British referendum on the European Constitutional Treaty. The Conservative Party has represented a wide swathe of British public opinion in asserting that this undertaking should logically be applied to the successor of the Constitutional Treaty, the Treaty of Lisbon. It is established Conservative policy that if their party becomes the British government before the Treaty of Lisbon has been ratified in all member states of the Union, the new Conservative government will hold a British referendum on the Treaty, in which the government will be urging a negative vote, on the ground that the Treaty represents an unacceptable deepening of British participation in the process of European integration.

While it is clear what the Conservative policy in government towards ratification will be if the fate of the Lisbon Treaty is still unresolved when the Conservatives come into office, the party has however been noticeably more equivocal about its approach to the Treaty if ratification has been completed in all member states of the Union before a hypothetical Conservative victory in the next British General Election. Mr. Cameron has been reluctant to promise a British referendum to withdraw the United Kingdom from a Treaty already ratified by all member states of the Union. He has contented himself with the vague formula that if the Conservative Party comes to power at a time when the Lisbon Treaty is already ratified and in force throughout the Union, it will 'not let matters rest.' It might well be that Mr. Brown will be able at the next General Election to create tactical difficulties for Mr. Cameron by pressing him on what exactly so imprecise an undertaking might mean in the reality of government. Within his own party, Mr. Cameron is by no means the most radical Eurosceptic, and Mr. Brown will certainly hope that divisions within the Conservative Party on the best approach to dealing with a Lisbon Treaty ratified in all member states can in due course be exploited to the benefit of his Labour government when it seeks reelection.

It would obviously be naïve to claim that in its European policy, Mr. Brown's is the only government of a member state in the Union which is motivated by domestic political considerations. Mr. Chirac's decision to hold a French referendum on the Constitutional Treaty was based in part upon his belief that the French

Socialist Party would be split in their assessment of the Treaty between advocates and opponents of the document, a split which did indeed occur, albeit at the cost of a rejection of the Treaty by the French electorate as a whole. Most political and even academic commentary on the European Elections every five years focusses on the domestic political impact of those elections at least as much as on their implications for the political balance of the European Parliament. It is no particular criticism of Mr. Brown to point to the domestic political considerations which encouraged him to ratify the Lisbon Treaty so rapidly after the unexpected outcome of the Irish referendum. It is, however, important for Britain's neighbours to understand that this rapid ratification is indeed a consequence of purely opportunistic and tactical considerations by the British government. It certainly implies no underlying change in British public, political or social attitudes to the European Union and the Constitutional or Lisbon Treaties.

When Mr. Blair became Prime Minister in 1997, he often echoed an initial aspiration of his predecessor, Mr. Major, to help the United Kingdom to feel 'more at ease' within the EU. In the years of his premiership from 1990 to 1997, Mr. Major signally failed in that aspiration, and it would be difficult to argue that Mr. Blair was notably more successful during his period of office. Mr. Major inherited from his predecessor, Mrs. Thatcher, a Conservative Party rapidly moving away from its traditionally sympathetic view of European integration and Britain's position within it. An important part of Mr.

Blair's electoral appeal in 1997 was his promise that he would pursue more constructive and co-operative policies within the European Union than had his ineffectual predecessor, Mr. Major. As Mr. Blair's premiership continued, the similarities between his European policies and those of Mr. Major became, however, daily more striking. An important reason why Mr. Blair's government was so willing to abandon the ratification procedure for the Constitutional Treaty in 2005 was its growing realization that the promised British referendum on this subject could not be won. The confidence with which Mr. Blair had originally approached his mission to make his fellow-citizens more content with their position in the European Union was almost entirely dissipated by that time. Indeed, the terms in which, two years after the effective death-knell of the European Constitutional Treaty, Mr. Blair and his colleagues approached the negotiations leading up to the signing of the Lisbon Treaty, with their rhetoric of 'red lines', opt-outs and special declarations, were hardly those of a self-confident government robustly determined to explain to the British electorate why further progress in European integration was in the long-term interest of all those participating in it.

When it still believed that it could win a referendum on the Constitutional Treaty, Mr. Blair's government considered a range of arguments to deploy which its advisers on public opinion recommended as likely to commend themselves to the British public. The argument that voting against the Constitutional Treaty would be the equivalent of voting to leave the European Union, an argument that might in the right circumstances have been an effective one, was nullified by the French and Dutch referendums, after which there was no suggestion that either France or the Netherlands might be compelled to leave the Union. More politically attractive at first glance was a related argument that the Constitutional Treaty represented no more than a ratification and systematization of existing practices and competences within the European Union, that should not be regarded as essentially deepening or developing the existing level of integration within the European Union. For an illuminating reason, Mr. Blair's government also concluded that this argument would carry little weight with the British electorate.

The blunt fact is that after more than twelve years of Mr. Blair's and Mr. Brown's stewardship, the degree of public emotional estrangement in the United Kingdom from the EU is, if anything, higher than it was in 1997. Much of British public opinion regards the present degree of European integration in which the United Kingdom participates as already being unacceptably high. Even if it could be demonstrated with absolute cogency that the Lisbon Treaty implied no greater level of integration than that currently in operation, it is doubtful whether a referendum could be won about the Treaty in the United Kingdom. But no such demonstration is possible. It is no doubt true that the new integrative momentum given to the EU by the Treaty of Lisbon is less than that given by, for instance, the Maastricht Treaty, but it is emphatically not a treaty which cuts back the existing level of European integration or blocks off all possibilities of future integrative development. To have any realistic possibility of being endorsed in a British popular referendum, both these unrealizable preconditions would have to be met. The Lisbon Treaty does not do so, and it is difficult to imagine that unanimity could ever be achieved among Britain's partners for the signing of a new European text which would meet these specifically British demands. Britain is today a semi-detached member of the EU, and yet this semi-detachment is for many in the United Kingdom an uncomfortably intimate European embrace. The Constitutional Treaty would have been, and the Lisbon Treaty would be subjected in any British referendum campaign to a depth of hostile scrutiny which few diplomatic texts could ever survive.

In truth, neither the Lisbon Treaty nor its predecessor, the European Constitutional Treaty, are documents well designed for the vigorous and simplified exchanges of national referendum campaign, be it in the United Kingdom, Spain or Luxembourg. They are pre-eminently texts written by and for experts, who understand that none of the paragraphs or even sentences of the treaties should be taken in isolation from each other, that sometimes agreement between 27 member states is only possible on the basis of ambiguity, and that impenetrable technical vocabulary is often desired by the signatories of treaties to conceal the significance of the concessions they are making or the triumphs they are achieving. Both the Constitutional and Lisbon Treaties have been criticized for lacking overarching themes, themes that would serve as the focal points of political campaigns to mobilize enthusiastic support among the general population called upon to vote in plebiscites. This absence is hardly surprising, given the wide spectrum of aspirations and interests which both treaties needed to accommodate, ranging from British immobilism to the radical integrationism of the Belgians and the Luxembourgers.

How precisely matters stand concerning the Lisbon Treaty at the end of 2009 will be a matter of some importance for British domestic politics, and therefore for the EU as a whole. It will be significant for the European choices of the probably incoming Conservative government in spring 2010 whether the Treaty is by the end of 2009 already ratified, already renounced or still in a state of suspended animation. It will be an important task of the Swedish Presidency in the latter part of the year to have plans prepared for dealing with any outcome of the Irish referendum, whether to press for countries that may have not yet ratified (probably Poland and the Czech Republic) urgently to do so, or to move rapidly to the abandonment of the Lisbon Treaty in the case of another vote of rejection from Ireland. If the Lisbon Treaty has neither been ratified, nor abandoned by the time of the British General Election in the first half of 2010, it is an inevitability that there will be a British referendum on the Treaty, with the government of the day urging a negative vote. A British referendum on the Lisbon Treaty which led to the Treaty's abandonment would be a profoundly destabilizing event both for the United Kingdom and for its European partners.

It is not at all clear, however, that such destabilization can be avoided, even in the event of the Lisbon Treaty's having entered into force before the Conservative Party comes to power. There is admittedly a widespread analysis (which can be regarded as optimistic or cynical, according to taste) among the British commentariat, which claims that Mr. Cameron, the leader of the Conservatives, would not be sorry to have the question of the ratification of the Lisbon Treaty resolved by the second Irish referendum and the Labour government in a manner which he can criticize, but then find himself unable to reverse when he comes to office. The commentators who adopt this view rightly point out that Mr. Cameron's hostility to the EU has been much less marked a feature of his political persona than it has been for other recent Conservative leaders. He will find no great difficulty, they predict, in moving his party once in government towards a less ideologically-tinged view of the EU. The realities of office will force upon him the necessity of consensual decision-making through the forging of alliances which is at the heart of the European decision-making process. The Conservative Party may not come to love Europe in government, but it will find itself working with its European partners in the structures of the EU, a collaboration which inevitably will have a socializing effect on even the most Eurosceptic Conservative minister.

This analysis may be correct, but another analysis is at least equally plausible. None of Mr. Cameron's expressed views on the EU are other than highly Eurosceptic, firmly in the mainstream of what his Conservative party now believes. His decision to talk less about the EU than did his predecessors is undoubtedly a largely tactical one, which may well be revised in the period leading up to the General Election predicted for 2010. Even in government, there will be many of Mr. Cameron's closest colleagues and advisers urging him to placate the notoriously unruly radical Eurosceptics of the Conservative Party by an unbridled attack on the provisions of the Lisbon Treaty. Renegotiation of the terms of British membership of the EU is anyway a long-standing goal of many senior Conservatives and their ardour will be increased rather than decreased by the in their view illegitimately ratified Lisbon Treaty and its (once again in their view) devastating consequences for the United Kingdom.

The question of whether the Conservative Party continues after the next European Elections to sit in the EPP Group of the European Parliament will be a revealing pointer towards the likely European policies of Mr. Cameron in government. In order to make his original candidature for the leadership of the Conservative Party more attractive to the most Eurosceptic of his Parliamentary colleagues, Mr. Cameron promised in 2005 that he would withdraw the Conservative MEPs from their parliamentary alliance in Strasbourg with the European People's Party. Since becoming leader of the Conservative Party, Mr. Cameron has not implemented this promise, much to the discontent of some among his original supporters. He has nevertheless promised to do so after the European Elections of 2009, a promise which there seems no reason to doubt that he will carry out. His willingness or otherwise after the European Elections to remove the

Conservative Party from the mainstream of centre-right politics and policies by abandoning the EPP is already widely seen as a touchstone of the European aspirations and expectations he will bring to his likely premiership.

It seems overwhelmingly likely that over the coming months public and political discussion in the United Kingdom about the Lisbon Treaty will not primarily focus on the terms of the Treaty itself. Those in the United Kingdom generally content with the present workings of the EU and with the United Kingdom's role within the EU will in their overwhelming majority favour the Lisbon Treaty, welcoming it with differing degrees of enthusiasm, ranging from the fervently evangelical to the barely accepting. Those in the United Kingdom who are not content with the present workings of the Union will find little in the Treaty of Lisbon to make the EU more acceptable from their point of view. As Eisenhower might have put it, the Treaty of Lisbon makes the EU more like itself than it was before. It does not turn the Union into what many British voters would like it to be, namely a loose trading arrangement with a minimum of institutional or political structures. Over the past decade, the realization has gained ground within the United Kingdom that the EU will never be changed in such a way as to correspond to a purely British view of its teleology. In the early years of his premiership at least, Mr. Blair was perhaps too willing to imply that such an objective was an achievable one. The growing consciousness that it was not has led to a corresponding disillusionment on the part of some Britons, a disillusionment not always directed at Mr. Blair for having misled them, but rather at the EU for being other than many British observers would wish it to be. In some moods, the British public prides itself upon its pragmatism, its realism and its intellectual flexibility. Mr. Blair's period as Prime Minister saw a distinct retrogression from all these values in British popular and political attitudes towards the EU. Public perceptions of the Lisbon Treaty have faithfully reflected this evolution. The apparent British debate about the Lisbon Treaty is not really one about that Treaty, but one about Britain's future position within the EU. If the British debate on the Lisbon Treaty is often confused and uncertain, it is because Britain's future position within the EU is confused and uncertain. It is difficult to believe that four or eight years of Conservative government will resolve this confusion and uncertainty. If they do, it can only logically be in the sense of further consolidating and perhaps cementing irreversibly Britain's current self-willed marginalization within the EU. Mr. Cameron has said that he does not wish to leave the EU. Even within the strict terms of this undertaking, the coming years of probable Conservative government may well serve to test a new paradigm of membership, that of formal British membership within the Union, combined with an ever more restricted application of the substance of this membership.

Muscles from Brussels: a 21st Century Superpower

Richard Whitman

Introduction

Before the end of the Cold War, in 1988, Professor Samuel Huntington wrote:

> The European Community, if it were to become politically cohesive, would have the population, resources, economic wealth, technology, and actual and potential military strength to be the preeminent power of the twenty-first century.

Huntington was prescient in identifying that the EU had the capacity to become a significant international actor but incorrect in the preconditions that he set. The EU has not become politically cohesive in the sense of transforming itself into a proto-European nation state, but rather (and what Huntington could not have fully identified then) the structure of international relations has been transforming to create an environment in which the forms of power that the EU exercises are of relatively greater significance.

The idea explored in this article is that it is the changing external context that has contributed to the increasing international importance of the Union and, in turn, the EU is itself contributing to these changes. To explore this idea, three areas of change in contemporary international relations are used to illustrate how these contribute to an increase in the *relative* international significance of the Union:

- the changing balance of power in the international system;
- the changing international political economy;
- and the increasing institutionalisation of international relations.

The Changing Balance of Power in International Relations

The bipolar balance of power, or bipolarity, has been frequently used to characterise the distribution of significant, and effective, world power in the international system that emerged in the aftermath of the Second World War. Two major contenders emerged – the United States and the Soviet Union – and the widespread alignment of nation-states to one or other of these two came to exemplify the balance of power of the international system of the post-war period.

It was from thinking about power, and the balance of power, that the term 'superpower' itself was coined in a book written in 1944 by William T.R. Fox, an American foreign policy professor. Fox used the term to identify a new category of power able to occupy the highest status in a world in which, as the war then raging demonstrated, states could challenge and fight each other on a global scale.

According to Fox, there were (at that moment) three states that were superpowers: the United States, the Soviet Union and Britain. The full title of his volume was *The Superpowers: The United States, Britain and the Soviet Union – Their Responsibility for Peace*. Fox's argument was that world peace was dependent on the ability of a few key powers upholding world order. A superpower was not just a monumentally powerful political community, but also one which was willing to stand up and be counted in assuming its special duties and obligations in the wider world.

Almost at the moment in which superpower was defined the third superpower disappeared.

So a tri-polar balance of power became a bipolar balance of power. And superpowers and a bipolar balance of power became synonymous with one another. For many commentators one of the characteristics of the bipolar system and the institutions and arrangements that characterised its development was its relative stability, understood as no direct war between the great powers in the system. However, there was a cost for this stability; one which was paid in what we then called the third world, with the superpowers pursuing conflict by proxy in Asia, Africa and Central and South America.

Having failed to predict the end of the Cold War, scholars have now spent almost 20 years trying to explain what has replaced it. The end of the Cold War raised many questions about the nature of the new international environment and what had replaced the bipolar balance of power.

In the late 1980s and early 1990s some – mostly US-based – analysts suggested that the international system had moved into a state of tripolarity with economic confrontation between the EU, US and Japan replacing power politics as the new ordering principle of the international system. The EU had 'arrived' as one of the pre-eminent actors of the international system in the late 20th Century. The talk was no longer just of Geo-politics but also of Geo-economics. The tools and instruments of commerce were viewed as replacing the accoutrements of war as measures of significant power in the international system. In the analysis of Joseph Nye, we had entered an era in which 'Soft Power' was displacing 'Hard Power'.

This notion of a rising geo-economics replacing a rising geopolitics was rather hastily pushed to one side with the invasion of Kuwait in August 1990 and outbreak of conflict in Yugoslavia in 1991 which appeared to reinstate the idea that to preserve peace within international relations there was the need to possess the means to use force – something which the European Union and its Member States did not possess collectively.

To some commentators across the Atlantic it appeared that we had reached a 'uni-polar moment' in which the United States exercised a pre-eminent military and political power as its old challenger the Soviet Union disintegrated and disappeared as an actor of significance within international relations. Hubert Védrine, the then French foreign minister, described the United States in 1999 as having surpassed the status of superpower to become a 'hyperpower'. It was also in that moment that some commentators across the pond decided that we had reached the End of History, giving rise to the idea that the 21st Century was to be the American century and sowing the seeds of what we came to know as neo-conservative thinking about the uses to which this power should be put.

Europeans bear a responsibility for the more hubristic elements of this US thinking. We collectively (and here I mean Western Europeans) sub-contracted our geopolitical thinking to the United States. Europeans lost their geo-political mojo during the cold war. Geopolitics was something we also associated with empire, and had not geopolitics and a concern with global predominance got Europeans into enough trouble during the 20th Century?

In the late noughties we have suddenly been confronted with the rather abrupt end of the *Pax Americana* which disappeared somewhere in the middle of the war in Iraq. The United States appeared to have lost not just the capability for its will to prevail militarily but also its authority and so its pretentions to a leadership role within international relations. These cannot be easily regained even by an intelligent and charismatic new US President.

All great powers are – eventually – surpassed. Paul Kennedy, in his masterly work of 1989 *The Rise and Fall of the Great Powers*, reminded us of the inter-relationship between economic wealth as the mainstay of military power and, in turn, military power as the best guarantee for the expansion and retention of economic strength.

This measure of the economic and military strength of one nation-state relative to others in the system provides a guide to the retention and elimination of great power status over the long-term. Kennedy also made the point that great powers exercise their power and influence by guaranteeing international peace and prosperity through creating and maintaining international rules and institutions – a role that in the discipline of international relations we have come to characterise as the exercise of hegemony.

There is now a degree of uncertainty as to the consequences of the decline of a US hegemony both for world order and the functioning of the international economy. There has been a great debate on this in the United States. There has been rather less debate in Europe as to what the implications are for us collectively.

International relations theorists are struggling to comprehend where we currently find ourselves. The view has been advanced that we are now confronted by a new concert of 'Great Powers' encompassing the so-called BRICs of Brazil, Russia, India and China in addition to the US, Japan and the EU.

The best we can say about this notion of a putative new concert of great powers is that they are, currently, a rather disparate and unequal grouping. The EU clearly has a claim to the top table. And the EU self-consciously calculates and publishes the capabilities of the EU in contrast to Japan, the US and BRICs by comparison of elements of their respective resource capabilities – geographical area; population; Gross Domestic Product; and Gross Domestic Product per head. In themselves, these measures provide no indication as to how these capabilities translate into political power in the international system but the distribution of these capabilities relative to other states raises questions about the balance of power in the contemporary international system.

Assessment of the trends of the development of these capabilities over the long-term is clearly crucial for discerning the changing distribution of relative capabilities of nation-states. However, for the purposes of this essay we are seeking to assess the contemporary international identity of the EU and this, inevitably, requires a snap-shot assessment of the EU relative to other putative great powers in the international system.

The EU may not yet be able to claim a grand geo-political role for itself, or even to be considered a cohesive actor in the international system, but it does possesses both the resource capabilities to make itself significant and the instruments through which to implement this.

Furthermore, there are increasing expectations being made of the EU and we are now aware, through a burgeoning area of research, that the political elite and publics in these other great powers have a strong sense of the EU's coherence and heightened expectations.

What conclusions can be drawn from this? Quite simply that measured across certain indices and when compared with states that are increasingly represented as the 'rising powers' the EU does not look out of place. I am not arguing that the EU is some kind of proto-19th Century great power engaged in balance of power with a collection of other states. This is primarily because the EU lacks *fungibility* – that is, the capacity to bring all of these capabilities to bear to further its interests. But with increasing globalisation and with its attendant regionalisation and institutionalisation, we are not travelling back to a 19th Century future but rather forward, to a world of international relations in which the position and role of putative great powers has been transformed.

The Changing International Political Economy

The rise of the BRICs has been generated by changes within the international political economy and primarily the *relative* decline of the US *vis-à-vis* other states and regions. This change has been a long time in the making and until recently has been rather masked by the predominant military power enjoyed by the US. The issue is not just one about the relative size of the US economy but also about the role and functions performed by the US within the international political economy. It has been remarked by many commentators that the EU's role as the world's leading trader and its share of world GDP make it an economic superpower.The key period of transformation for the EEC/EU actually took place through the 1960s and 1970s when America's Cold War allies Japan and the EEC, sheltering under the US security umbrella, moved away from relations of economic dependency to economic capabilities that increased their assertiveness and independence. In 1960, EEC and Japanese output did not surpass that of the US. By the late 1980s this situation had been dramatically reversed with the then EC becoming a comparable challenger to US economic pre-eminence.

The EU currently accounts for the largest share of world GDP. It is the world's leading trader in goods and services and trade occupies a greater proportion of GDP than that for either the US or Japan. The EU is an unquestionably important player within the international political economy. What is as important is the trend in the international political economy in which the EU's relative share of world trade is falling at a much slower rate than that of the US.

US economic decline has also given rise to a debate about hegemony and the status of hegemonic power in the international system. The notion of hegemony as used by international political economists refers to a state that enjoys preponderant power in terms of production, markets and capital, as well as competitive advantages in those goods which are especially valued and involve the use of new and complex technologies. From this resource power, a hegemon is in a position to make, sustain and enforce the rules of the world political economy. The US has been increasingly forced to share this role with the EU across the last three decades.

In turn the EU has become a much more important rule-setter in the international political economy by virtue of the size and importance of its economy but also importantly since the process of creating the European single market began. The norms and standards set for the single market have increasingly been adopted by third parties, due to the size of the single market and the need to comply with its rules as destination for exports of goods and services. Consequently, EU product, health and safety and regulatory standards have been adopted 'off the shelf' by states across the world.

Furthermore, the EU has been able to carve out a role as rule-setter and rule-promoter in the area of responses to climate change and the politics of the environment as the US has abrogated a leadership role in this area for the last decade and a half.

The situation of relative US decline has opened up a debate on hegemony, its loss and appropriate responses. To put the dilemma in crude terms, will the Chinese, Indians and Brazilians be content to see the international political economy run through the G8, the WTO, the World Bank and the IMF with the voting rights, rules and procedures as they currently operate?

Within the founding treaties that created the ECSC, EEC and Euratom, a single supranational entity was created with broad authority over all aspects of trade relations between member states and the rest of the world. The internal integration process drove an external predisposition towards multilateralism: it became a part of the Community's political DNA. Member States were thus able to present themselves as a single bloc in international negotiations with other actors such as the US, or to participate in GATT rounds by presenting a single voice, with the European Commission in the driving seat in defining policy and as the prime negotiator.

Arrangements have become more challenging for the EU as more recent rounds of trade negotiations have focused on trade in services and on intellectual property, topics not fully anticipated in the founding Treaties. The locus of research in this field now increasingly focuses on how the EU negotiates and represents itself across the range of organisations and agencies that touch upon the definition of international rules and norms.

Alongside this multilateral diplomacy, in the last 50 years the EEC, EU and now EU has established a network of economic relations with most non-member countries. At first sight, the EU record shows an impressive number of trade agreements, in the form of preferential trade agreements, cooperation agreements, association agreements, etc. These arrangements bilaterally regulate economic relations between the EU and non-members, with a varying degree of preferential treatment accorded. The EU has 'painted the map blue', as it is easier to list the countries with which the EU does not have a trade agreement than to list those with which it does have an agreement.

For many trade policy does not represent foreign policy. However, what the EU has done across time is to seek additionality by moving to include political clauses about democracy, human rights and nuclear disarmament, which are an integral part to the agreements it concludes with others and constitute the basis for political dialogues and assessments of the political situations in third countries.

Foreign economic policy has been a testing ground for the EU in developing a distinctive form of diplomacy. The

EU has moved from bilateral or multilateral agreements dealing with purely trade or development policies to agreements with a much more explicit political intent such as the European Neighbourhood Policy which groups together all the states that neighbour the EU in Eastern Europe and the Mediterranean littoral for the purpose of transforming their economies and stimulating political liberalisation. The development of these sets of relationships, for example with former colonies in Africa, the Caribbean and the Pacific in the 1970s and with Latin America in the 1980s, has often been stimulated by the enlargement of the EU.

It is this strength of the EU deriving from its economy and its role in the international political economy that has given rise to a body of literature that asserts that the EU has already achieved superpower status. John McCormick, for example, has argued this case, based on the size and global reach of the EU's economy and the global political influence that this brings. McCormick's argument is that the nature of power has changed since the cold war-driven definition of superpower was developed, and that military power is no longer essential to great power; he argues that control of the means of production is more important than control of the means of destruction.

The Euro

There is also one other area of importance in the international political economy which the EU has chipped away at the hegemonic position occupied by the United States and that is with the emergence of the Euro as a currency of international significance alongside the dollar. The Euro has indeed become the second most important international currency after the US dollar.

There are even more Euro notes and coins in circulation than dollars and this is not because the European Central back has pursued a policy of quantitative easing. The Euro's international prominence clearly surpasses that of the Japanese yen and the pound sterling. With the present exchange rates, the Euro area GDP is higher than that of the United States. Euro-denominated international debt accounts for almost 49 per cent of the outstanding stock of international bonds and notes. In global foreign exchange markets, the Euro is the second most actively traded currency after the US dollar. The Euro-dollar currency pair is the most actively traded pair in global foreign exchange markets, and it accounts for more than one-quarter of global turnover. Data on the currency composition of global foreign exchange reserves show that the Euro now accounts for more than 26 per cent.

However, for EU external action to be truly effective, Euro area representation would appear to need to move from fragmentation to consolidation in the IMF and G groups. This would strengthen the Euro area's negotiating power and reduce the costs of international coordination.

Such a streamlined set of arrangements might be viewed as the logical consequence of the process of economic and monetary integration and would certainly have helped the Euro area play its fuller role in the resolution of current global economic challenges. However, it is only one half of the EMU's unfinished business. The other is an enhanced governance system within EMU that would allow Euro area countries to streamline policy positions and speak with a common voice on global issues.

The Increasing Institutionalisation of International Relations

The third strand of my argument is that it is the increasing institutionalisation of international relations and the EU's response to that institutionalisation that provides for me a distinctive component of the EU's international role.

The period since the birth of the United Nations has seen an acceleration in the creation of international and regional organisations. The current Yearbook of International Organizations lists over 7,000 intergovernmental international and regional organizations alone. There has been a substantial increase in regionalism, with intergovernmental and non-governmental organisations set up to encompass different regions of the globe and to incorporate a variety of tasks. The EU, itself a manifestation of a particular kind of regionalism in the international system, has developed the institutions of governance, incomplete as they are, to exercise power alongside and above the nation-state.

The widespread recognition of the increasing blurring of the domestic and the international through the rising interdependence of nation states, has called into question the viability of state sovereignty and the exercise of state power internationally. The impact of the transnational pressures of demography and accompanying environmental and technological changes have raised questions about the future of the nation state as a form of political organisation and its ability to cope with a new security agenda driven by global imperatives and challenges.

And so a 'bifurcated' global system, with a state-centric world coexisting and competing with a multi-centric world of transnational, national and subnational actors, is upon us. The EU is the exemplification of these developments, with the disaggregation of power between the Member States and the European Union and their co-existent relationship placing the EU simultaneously within the state-centric and the multi-centric world of post-international politics.

Europe has led the field in these developments in that the continent is characterised by the unique density of international institutions covering it. We have the OSCE, Council of Europe, NATO. These pan-European institutions operate alongside a significant number of sub-regional organisations in Europe. As the EU has enlarged, its member states represent an increasing share of the membership of all of these organisations. The EU is something of a cuckoo in the nest.

It is this very embeddedness of European states within multilateral and regional organisations that provides an important part of the DNA of Europe's global role. Europeans have a built-in predisposition to approach international relations through institutions and favour the creation of international regimes and norms. Europeans wish to domesticate international relations and do not see international institutions as fetters on their international relations. This creates a distinctive characteristic to European policy. It was also at the heart of intra-European disputes over the response to the war in Iraq. The Bush administration sought to cajole and seduce European governments into a policy that short-circuited or subverted the role and function of the collective security arrangements of the United Nations.

If we turn to international organisations outside Europe the picture is more mixed in terms of the capacity of the EU to punch its weight. If we take the United Nations Security Council and the G8 as illustrations, a much more complicated arrangement of representation takes place: one in which collective representation by the EU has proved to be rather problematic and one might say serves to dissipate EU power and influence. Furthermore, it is not unreasonable to assume that the increasing pressure by the BRICs for realigned membership of these two entities will place the EU under pressure to streamline its representation. Might it be better for the EU to come to a view as to what would be a more agreeable form of representation?

Where the EU has more of a problem is not in understanding the value of multilateralism, but rather in exercising power and influence within multilateral institutions in a manner that is commensurate with its collective capabilities. This takes us to attempts by the EU member states to create a more coherent foreign policy alongside their foreign economic policy.

Attempts by European states to formulate a collective foreign policy have been in existence for nearly 40 years, originally driven in response to US foreign policy at the time, and Europe's desire to act as a 'Second Western Voice'. Some commentators have taken the view that this has been more about creating ways to talk about foreign policy than actually making it – in the words of one commentator 'Procedure as a Substitute for Policy' – or, less charitably, EU foreign policy fiddling while Sarajevo, Beirut, Georgia, or Gaza City burns.

The policy-making process operates under a set of principles that largely remain unchanged today: it is consultative and collaborative, operating by unanimous agreement rather than voting determining policy; it is based on the principle of intergovernmentalism (that is that the member states remain in the driving seat) rather than giving the leading role to the European Commission and adjudication to the European Court of Justice or the power to determine priorities to the European Parliament; and it operates alongside national foreign policy – that is, the member states retain the means and right to pursue national foreign policies.

In the early 1990s, the EU reformulated its foreign policy coordination approach with the creation of the Common Foreign and Security Policy (CFSP). While the broad principles have remained unchanged since then, there have been two substantial developments. The first is that the member states have created a greater number of instruments and arrangements through which they collectively implement foreign policy. The second is that over time they have found it possible to reach a consensus on a number of specific foreign policy issues and to codify that consensus, so we can now identify a portfolio of European foreign policy.

Successive amendments to the CSFP under the Maastricht Treaty of 1991, the Amsterdam Treaty of 1999 and the Nice Treaty of 2003 have given greater form and function to the collective European foreign policy in this sense.

The EU now has its own High Representative for Common Foreign and Security Policy, Javier Solana, the public face and chief animator of European diplomacy alongside the rotating six-monthly EU Presidency. The EU also has Special Representatives responsible for the EU's approach to trouble spots and unresolved conflicts.

Europe has developed a range of instruments to pursue foreign policy, from sanctions and election monitoring to policing missions in third countries and taking on the role of governor, or imperial viceroy for Bosnia and Kosovo. We also have a range of collective foreign policy positions through so-called joint actions and common positions that address almost the entire range of international issues. All of this implemented through a rather modest budget of Euro 100 million.

In practice, the EU's decision-making instruments often prove to be rather too inflexible, given the fast-paced decision-making required in response to international developments and crises. Each Member State has retained its own foreign minister, foreign ministry and foreign aid budget. The EU does not possess the normal accoutrements that we expect for a foreign policy in that it does not possess a foreign ministry nor diplomatic missions in third countries, although important changes will take place to modify this situation if the Lisbon Treaty is ratified.

The EU often still falls back on bland statements in response to foreign policy crises. But across time we have seen joint actions and common positions used much more frequently – for example, to impose economic, diplomatic and other sanctions on third countries, or to set out the EU's stance on particular topics. Until fairly recently these resembled the manner in which children play with lego: the tendency to create larger and larger rather formless lumps of bricks.

This comes back to my earlier point about the absence of a European geo-political gene. Creating an over-arching narrative for this foreign policy has proved to be rather difficult. I think this is primarily because European governments have been unwilling to recognise the potential power and influence that they possess collectively.

There have been modest and cautious moves to correct this weakness, particularly the EU's first 'European Security Strategy', agreed by the EU's Heads of State and Government in December 2003. President Barack Obama will shortly issue the new US equivalent, and although the EU document is somewhat less ambitious (and shorter) it does have the same basic intention, which is to set out where the existential threats to European security lie and how these might be countered. The policy response to these threats is to make multilateral institutions better at dealing with them – 'effective multilateralism' – and to seek a set of deepened relationships with a set of strategic partners.

This commitment to 'effective multilateralism' is the closest we have to an organising principle or tenet of

European foreign policy. It is not a bad governing principle as it encapsulates what the EU is; it sets out its default mode of operation; and it also provides a guide to what it wants – more institutionalisation of international relations, and global public policy problems to be dealt with through institutionalised, negotiated structures and processes. In short, it wants to remake the world in its own image.

On its own doorstep the EU has done this more assertively through the policy of enlargement. This is, for many commentators, its strongest foreign policy tool. Through its policy of enlargement the EU has transformed the international relations of Europe. For those familiar with the more recent variants of the Star Trek franchise the EU resembles 'the Borg' that is the nemesis of Captain Jean Luc Picard, in that resistance to membership appear futile as the EU absorbs the countries on its borders with whom it comes into contact. Enlargement has been a continuous project of the EU since the early 1990s in either negotiating membership or assimilating new members.

The process of EU enlargement has also given rise to the question of whether the EU itself is an imperial entity by the pattern of its growth. Our three superpowers were also empires. And the EU does have some of the characteristics of imperial endeavour in maintaining its expansion on the basis of co-option, consent and a degree of coercion.

Getting Muscular: Military Power

So far one aspect of superpower on which Fox put some emphasis has been side-stepped in this piece, which is that of military power. That is, the capacity to, as Fox put it, 'fight each other on a global scale'.

For most European states the Cold War was a period in which they did not face, or did not possess, the capability to determine how and for what purposes military power was used. It was for that reason that the European Union was described as a 'Civilian Power' by academics – the most enduring concept that we had to characterise the international role played by the EU.

Being a civilian power is not the same thing as being a pacifist power, and collectively European states possess substantial military capabilities. If we take a look at the International Institute for Strategic Studies's *Military Balance*, the annual assessment of military forces and defence expenditures, the European Union does not warrant an entry on its capabilities. And this is quite simply because the EU does not possess any armed forces of its own – but then neither does NATO which is composed of forces made available by its member states.

If we aggregate the armed forces of the EU member states and then compare the defence budget and active armed forces for the EU Member States, the US, Japan, China and Russia we arrive at an interesting outcome. The figures place the combined active armed forces of the EU Member States second only to the figure claimed for China and the combined defence expenditure of the 27, second only to the figure claimed for the US.

The presentation of such data represents no comment upon the capabilities, force posture or defence policy of those under comparison.

EU member states also do not have a problem in sending their armed forces overseas – all member states currently have their military deployed overseas. But they deploy them for specific purposes, with the majority deployed under NATO auspices or engaged in peacekeeping operations.

Until 1991, and the Maastricht Treaty, defence was a taboo subject for the European Community/Union. The Maastricht Treaty was an important change. The then 12 Member States set themselves the objective of having a common defence policy which might, in time, lead to a common defence.

Since the turn of the century things have moved (in EU terms) at a lightning pace. A European Union Security and Defence Policy (ESDP) has been created and the EU has moved from the position of being best characterised as a civilian power – albeit one with military aspirations – to an entity which now has the capacity to deploy military force and, while not having its own troops, with member states' armed forces deployed under the EU banner in operations beyond its boundaries.

As one can see from the map of the EU's military endeavours to date, the EU has deployed troops in sub-Saharan Africa and South Eastern Europe and replaced the SFOR operation in Bosnia. These operations encompass what are known as the 'Petersberg' tasks of humanitarian and rescue tasks, peacekeeping tasks and tasks of combat forces in crisis management, including peacemaking. The majority of the operations have not been large, but the number, duration and frequency of these deployments is increasing.

In addition the EU now has standby military forces called Battlegroups. There are now two Battlegroups on constant standby each consisting of around 1500 troops, ready to deploy within 15 days of a crisis, primarily in support of the UN, and normally for a period of around 30 days.

The Battlegroups are a staging post on the way to meeting the '2010 Headline Goal' set in 1999, which is to have a force made up of 60,000 troops capable of staying in the field for at least one year with all the necessary command and control, intelligence and strategic transport needed to sustain that presence.

The consequence of this goal is that the EU member states collectively need to provide 200,000 military personnel to facilitate the rotation of troops if active service was to be sustained for that time period.

These forces are to pursue the Petersberg tasks and not for invasion purposes. But crucially the guiding ethos is that the EU should have autonomous capacity to take decisions and, where NATO as a whole is not engaged, to launch and then to conduct EU-led military operations in response to international crises in support of the CFSP. What this means is that Europeans are developing a military capability to act independently from the United States.

Underpinning these arrangements is that individual EU member state defence ministries and militaries are going through a rethinking and restructuring process to participate in all of these processes.

An important adjunct of these developments is what has been happening in terms of defence industry consolidation and collaborative defence procurement. While this is a fascinating topic, it is beyond the scope of this essay. But my conclusion is that Europe also possesses the defence industrial base to sustain a top-flight military.

Europeans possess all that is necessary to become a military superpower – including a nuclear weapons capability – but have not collectively embarked upon the road to global military pre-eminence. Rather, we have had other priorities for our taxes. If a significant 'existential threat' was to emerge might this position be modified?

Towards a Pax Bruxellana?

I have outlined a whole series of ways in which the EU matters in international relations. I have suggested that the changes in the environment of international relations might also be working in Europe's favour; that the EU possesses the potential for a distinctive foreign policy; and that it has developed a set of instruments to pursue a form of diplomacy.

Europe will be internationally important even if it does not seek superpower status. It is a major part or sub-system of a wider international politics from which it cannot be separated. Europe contributes to over a quarter of global economic activity and is significant in the global political economy and the politics of the global environment. Europe is also affected by a variety of transnational and transborder phenomena that encompass migration, crime, and public health and that have widened the range of issues that are now the subject of international politics and with which states need to grapple. Pursuing a policy of isolationism is not an option for Europeans, nor for the EU.

To return to the subtitle of Fox's work in which he introduced the notion of superpower – *Their Responsibility for Peace*.

Europeans may possess the means but do they possess the will to take on the responsibilities of a 21st Century superpower? As the difficulties associated with the ratification of the Constitutional and Lisbon Treaties illustrate, publics are not necessarily persuaded that more powers for the European Union are a good thing. The Lisbon Treaty does contain some modest enhancements of the manner in which the EU would conduct its foreign, security and defence policies but they do not represent the step-change that would suddenly propel the EU into a greater player within international relations.

But becoming a superpower in the sense in which we understood superpower in the second half of the 20th Century – nuclear armed states engaged in a global military, economic and ideological contestation – is neither desirable nor feasible for the EU.

What is really needed is a new form of superpower, more suitable to the global challenges that will confront us in the 21st Century.

So what might this 21st Century superpower look like?

First, it needs to have a global reach in terms of its economy and finance, and to play a role in the definition and management and rules of the global economy and the international monetary system.

Second, it needs to have a capacity, and crucially a willingness, to take on a responsibility for actively managing and preserving international security by dealing with all the military, economic, societal and environmental existential threats that it faces.

Third, it needs a commitment to a set of norms and values that put a premium on solving the problems of human security and the common challenges that confront us globally, and a willingness to take the lead in solving these challenges, even where they have a domestic political and economic cost.

I have attempted to assert that Europeans collectively have the capacity to be a new, 21st Century superpower – we already have the muscles in Brussels.

But whether we want to play this role – to create a *Pax Bruxellana* – is another matter.

All the Member States of the Union, and particularly the larger Member States, will need to ask themselves this question in coming years. I have already hinted that these larger Member States can often find themselves torn between the theory of European solidarity and the reality of national interests. It is worth stressing in conclusion that this schizophrenia is by no means confined to the United Kingdom. In its sometimes uncertain approach to the building of a more muscular Brussels, the United Kingdom is firmly in the uncertain European mainstream. Those who live longest will know most about the eventual scope and destination of this mainstream.

www.ingramcontent.com/pod-product-compliance
Lightning Source LLC
LaVergne TN
LVHW090947080826
845145LV00003B/917

* 9 7 8 0 9 5 5 4 9 7 5 9 9 *